Classic cakes and bakes are given a face-lift in Stacie Bakes. Whatever the season or occasion, there's a new twist on an old favourite to suit. For those avoiding butter, Stacie turns carrot cake into Skinny carrot meringue cake; for Valentine's Day, chocolate gets a makeover with Salted caramel custard and chocolate cake; and for the autumn she turns up the volume on ginger cake with spicy Red mist cake with a pecan brandy sauce. She adds banana and chocolate to Baked Alaska, gives brownies the star treatment with Hazelnut meringue and brownie layer cake and creates a White forest gâteau, rich in white chocolate, cherries and cream. Retro and vintage tea party favourites are here too, from Fruit scones to Fondant fancies and a strawberry-and-cream-filled Victoria sandwich. Whether it's Valentine's Day or Mother's Day, Easter or Christmas, there are cakes, breads, pastries, bars, biscuits and even savouries to get you baking!

STACIE BAKES

Photography by Dan Jones

First published in the United Kingdom in 2013 by
PAVILION BOOKS
10 Southcombe Street
London
W14 0RA

An imprint of Anova Books Company Ltd

Text © Stacie Stewart 2013
Design and layout © Anova Books 2013
Photography © Dan Jones 2013 (excluding pages 7, 23, 30, 118, 205)
Photography © Helen Russell 2013 pages 7, 23, 30, 118, 205

Senior commissioning editor: Becca Spry
Cover design & art direction: Georgina Hewitt
Photographer: Dan Jones
Design: Karin Fremer
Copy editor: Maggie Ramsay
Stylist: Lucy Harvey
Food stylist: Emma Marsden
Production: Laura Brodie

ISBN: 9781909108066

A CIP catalogue record for this book is available from the British Library.
10 9 8 7 6 5 4 3 2 1
Repro by Rival Colour Ltd, UK
Printed by Toppan Leefung Printing Ltd, China

Cook's note: both metric and imperial measures are given for the recipes. Follow either set of measures, not a mixture of both, as they are not interchangeable. Medium eggs should be used except where otherwise specified. Free-range eggs are recommended. Note that some recipes contain raw or lightly cooked eggs. The young, elderly, pregnant women and anyone with an immune-deficiency disease should avoid these, because of the slight risk of salmonella.

Stacie Stewart

STACIE BAKES

Classic cakes and bakes for the thoroughly modern cook

Photography by Dan Jones

PAVILION

For my granda Ernie
28 July 1930 – 9 October 2012

You made the worst fried
breakfast in Sunderland but you
could make a skateboard out of a
hoover – nobody's perfect! xx

Contents

◆◆

Hello & welcome!

I've always known I would end up as a baker. Almost as soon as my nine cousins and I could walk, my Nana Jean taught us the basics of baking. I would stand on a stool at her kitchen table in her house in Carley Road, Sunderland. It didn't feel like a lesson; it was like playing a game, and with a few dozen mouths to feed around the family table, we provided extra pairs of hands willing to knead, roll and shape. This is where my love for proper, old-fashioned British baking began.

Classic baking, to me, means not only looking back to our baking heritage and continuing to bake and share those recipes, but also putting a modern spin on old classics. The Chocasheek (page 144), for example, is based on a cornflake cake that my Nana Jean has been making since before I was born; my mam remembers being given this cake on a Saturday afternoon, smothered in jam; I make it as a dessert, with a chocolate topping. In the past there was a sweet treat for every occasion and to suit every budget. Whatever the celebration – Valentine's, Easter, Mother's Day, school fêtes or Christmas – a cake seemed to be at the heart of it.

When I left school, I didn't have the confidence to go to catering college, so I followed my friends into university. It wasn't until I finished my degree that I realized my pastime was not only my passion but also my gift, and that I wanted to cook full time. At first I kept my job at a local supermarket, where I had worked to pay my way through university, but I always baked and cooked on the side. Paydays were the main event for me: I treated myself to one new cookbook a month and cooked for my mam and her friends: anything they wanted, but nearly always a three-course meal from my new set of recipes. It was an amazing time, when I honed my skills and learnt

about weird and wonderful things. You'd never believe it, but there's an encyclopedia of flour, and I've read it!

It wasn't until I was working in an office in Newcastle a few years later that I finally felt confident enough to follow my dream. In January 2010 I entered MasterChef. I came fourth after, believe it or not, messing up my dessert – a dessert you can try for yourself (page 131). Believe me, it's going to come out 10 times better than my version on MasterChef!

You don't have to be the greatest baker in the world to cook the recipes in this book, you just have to be prepared to have fun. And remember, the beneficiaries of your delights will be so warmed by being given a home-baked treat that they'll overlook any imperfections in how it looks. There's a section of baking tips you can refer to if you get stuck (page 10). If you make a cake and it looks rubbish, or it's sunk, just make sure you knock up a cracking icing to cover it; it'll still taste great. Think of a 'mistake cake' as yourself after a night out, and then think of the icing as 'a facial, two litres of water and make-up' – camouflage, baby!

Look at this book as your new kitchen best friend. It'll make you a domestic genius for all occasions: indulgent days, birthdays, summer holidays and cosy days with your mates. The chapters are divided into seasons and occasions, so no matter what time of the year, whatever is in season or what's happening in your social calendar, you'll have an abundance of recipes to try.

Enjoy this book, these stories and these recipes. They are from the heart – from me and my family to you and yours.

Baking tips

◆ **Always use medium, free-range eggs and unsalted butter** for the recipes in this book, unless otherwise specified.

◆ **Bring all cold ingredients, such as butter, milk and eggs, to room temperature** before use (about an hour out of the fridge is usually fine), unless otherwise specified.

◆ **Always sift plain white and self-raising flour** before use (it really does make a lot of difference to the lightness of the cake) and weigh the flour again after sifting.

◆ **Toast nuts before you use them** as it gives them much more flavour. If they are still in their skins, it loosens the skins and makes them easy to remove. To toast them, simply pop them in a dry, hot frying pan and cook over a medium heat for 5 minutes, until the skins or nuts begin to colour. Alternatively, pop them on a baking sheet and toast in a very hot oven for 5 minutes, but watch them like a hawk as they burn very quickly. Remove the skins by rubbing the nuts in a clean tea towel. You can always cheat and buy ready-toasted nuts, but they are slightly more expensive.

◆ **Throughout the book there are tips on how to make the most of your baking.** Little thing, such as how long you beat a cake batter for, how you roll your pastry and the temperature of your hands when rubbing in can make a big difference to the end result. It's these tips that took me from being a home baker to running my own business; they're what take my cakes from good to great.

◆ **In some recipes I've suggested variations**, and please feel free to swap fruits, nuts or spices for others if it sounds good to you. Improvising is how you learn and gain confidence; I'm here to teach and inspire, so work your magic.

Cake-making tips

◆ **Oven temperatures vary**: my mother's oven is about 20 years old and only really cooks things that are in the back left. If your oven is old, you probably know its ways, so use your judgement. The following tests will make sure your cakes are cooked properly.

◆ The cake should look firm on top, not wobbly or liquid, and it should be a nice golden colour.

◆ Insert a small, sharp knife, thin skewer or cocktail stick/ toothpick into the centre of your cake and then pull it out. If it comes out clean the cake is cooked, but if it comes out with mixture sticking to it, the cake is still raw in the centre, so pop it back in the oven for 4 minutes, then check it again. Repeat until the knife comes out clean.

◆ **Open the oven door for as short a time as possible when you put the cake in** and when you check it. Opening the door reduces the temperature of the oven, so the longer you open it for, the more likely it is that your cake won't cook in time. When testing whether your cake is done, open and close the door gently, being as quick as you can with the knife or skewer test.

◆ **If a cake is colouring too quickly**, cover the top with foil to speed up the cooking and prevent it from browning further.

◆ **Cool a cake in the tin on a wire rack** for 10 minutes before removing it from the tin. The wire rack (I use a shelf out of the oven) lets the air circulate under the cake, ensuring that it cools evenly.

◆ **Always ensure the cake is cool before handling or decorating it**, to avoid crumbing or breakage.

◆ **Don't be put off if you don't have the specified tin size**; just improvise. If a recipe calls for a 23cm/9in tin and you only have a 20cm/8in one, then just cook it for a little bit longer as the cake will be deeper. If you have a smaller loaf tin than the recipe calls for, simply halve the recipe or make two cakes. A great tip is to buy disposable foil containers, which are readily available from most supermarkets.

◆ **Lining and greasing tins** is an essential part of cake-making. Even the best non-stick tins can stick, so take an extra minute to make sure your tins are greased thoroughly and lined with baking parchment or greaseproof paper. Some recipes call for the bottom of the tin to be lined: to do this, put the tin on the parchment, draw around the bottom of the tin and cut the parchment out before you start baking. To line the sides, put a length of string around the tin to measure how much parchment you'll need to cut. Some tins are an awkward shape, so to prevent sticking they should be greased lightly but thoroughly and then coated with flour, tapping out any excess, instead of lining with parchment. There's nothing worse than spending an hour baking a cake and then finding that the top has stuck to the oven, making a massive hole – although if this does happen just fill it with icing!

◆ **Equipment**: when I learned to bake we had very little equipment. My Nana Jean always says 'all you need is a bowl and your hands pet', and that is how I learned – hands-on, no frills. Nana Jean tells tales of peeling potatoes with a blade my granda then used to shave with. This was working-class baking, in the days when she baked to feed six kids, herself and my granda. It wasn't a great pleasure as it is now; she had to work out ways to make small amounts of ingredients go a long way. Pastry featured heavily, being simple and cheap to make, especially as she used lard and water. Nowadays there seems to be a gadget or piece of equipment for everything, and baking has moved on from necessity to pleasure.

My baking terms

• **Beat, whisk and whip**: a vigorous method of incorporating ingredients. Butter and sugar are beaten together in many recipes; use a food mixer with the paddle attachment, an electric hand-whisk, or a wooden spoon if you're feeling energetic. Egg whites are whipped until thick and snowy; use a food mixer with the whisk attachment, an electric hand whisk or a balloon whisk.

• **Fold in**: a slow method of incorporating ingredients, which is less severe than beating. Whipped egg whites or cream are folded into heavier mixtures to keep as much air as possible. Use a large metal spoon or thin spatula and a gentle cutting and lifting movement to combine the two mixtures.

• **Crumb coat**: for professional-looking cakes that have a stiff buttercream icing, I recommend a 'crumb coat'. Once your cake has cooled and you have filled it ready for decorating, spread a very thin layer of buttercream all over the top and sides of the cake, to ensure the cake is essentially 'sealed', so that when you add your top layer of buttercream it goes on perfectly and you don't get any crumbs. You can leave your crumb-coated cake for up to a day before you finish decorating it, as long as it's stored in an airtight container.

Kitchen kit

These are the items I couldn't live without. Some are essential, others are luxuries.

- ◆ Proper measuring spoons: they cost very little and are essential for accuracy and consistency. There is a big difference between what you think a teaspoonful looks like and what it actually is.
- ◆ Kitchen scales: electronic digital scales give absolute precision, which is so important in baking.
- ◆ Spatulas and wooden spoons.
- ◆ A food mixer such as a KitchenAid, or at the very least, an electric hand-whisk.
- ◆ A food processor such as a Magimix: a good brand and a worthwhile investment.
- ◆ A rolling pin, not just for rolling pastry, but also for crushing biscuits and nuts. A wooden one will last a lifetime, but I love my silicone one because nothing sticks to it.
- ◆ A selection of tins, preferably with a loose bottom. 20cm/8in is the most commonly used; get a square and a round one.
- ◆ A tart tin: 23cm/9in is the size most recipes call for.
- ◆ Disposable foil containers are a great invention, and most supermarkets stock them. A useful size is 33 x 20cm/13 x 8in: perfect for brownies and other tray bakes.
- ◆ A 900g/2lb loaf tin; mine measures about 23 x 13cm/ 9 x 5in.
- ◆ A blowtorch makes caramelizing sugar for a glazed lemon tart or crème brûlée quick and easy.

Sweet pastry case

◆◆

This makes a blind-baked sweet pastry case, ready to use in various recipes in the book. You can make a standard shortcrust pastry by omitting the sugar. It's essential to keep everything as cold as possible when making pastry, especially the butter. The cold butter expands when it hits the heat of the oven, creating layers and a short, crisp pastry.

**MAKES 1 X 23CM/9IN
ROUND PASTRY SHELL**

◆ 200G/7OZ/GENEROUS 1½ CUPS
  PLAIN (ALL-PURPOSE) FLOUR
◆ 25G/1OZ/2 TBSP CASTER (SUPERFINE)
  SUGAR (OMIT FOR PLAIN SHORTCRUST),
  PLUS EXTRA FOR DUSTING
◆ 100G/3½OZ/7 TBSP UNSALTED
  BUTTER, COLD AND CUBED
◆ 1 EGG YOLK
◆ ICE-COLD WATER

1. You can make pastry by hand, in a food processor or a mixer. To make it by hand, put the flour, sugar (omit for plain shortcrust) and butter into a bowl. Using your fingertips, lightly rub it together until it resembles breadcrumbs. Alternatively, put these in a food processor and pulse, or use a mixer with the paddle attachment. It shouldn't take more than 2 minutes, or 5 by hand.

2. Add the egg yolk and as much ice-cold water as you need to bind the mixture to a soft dough. Gently squeeze together, mix in the processor or blend briefly. You don't want it to be too dry. If anything, it's better slightly sticky, as you can remedy this with a little flour when rolling out. Wrap the dough in cling film or in a plastic bag and pop it in the fridge for 30 minutes to relax.

3. Preheat the oven to 190°C/375°F/gas mark 5. Lightly grease a 23cm/9in diameter tart tin.

4. Scatter flour lightly over a work surface and flatten the pastry dough lightly with your hands. Flour your rolling pin and begin to roll out the pastry. Always roll backwards and forwards, never side to side, moving the pastry frequently to make sure it hasn't stuck.

5. When the pastry is roughly 3mm/⅛in thick and 25cm/10in in diameter you can line your tart tin. Pick up the pastry by rolling it loosely it around your rolling pin, then unrolling it over the tart tin. Leaving the pastry hanging over the sides, gently press it down into the sides and bottom of the tin. You should have plenty of slack on your pastry, so try not to stretch it. Don't worry if it tears; just patch it up with more pastry pressed over the torn bit.

RECIPE CONTINUES OVERLEAF

RECIPE CONTINUED FROM PREVIOUS PAGE

6. Place the pastry case in the fridge for 5 minutes. Cut a piece of greaseproof paper about 25cm/10in in diameter.

7. Remove the pastry case from the fridge and line it with the greaseproof paper, then fill the paper with dried beans. They should be tightly packed and fill the case to the brim: this prevents the sides of the case from sinking as you bake the pastry.

8. Bake for 15 minutes. Take the tin out of the oven and carefully remove the paper and beans. If there are any tears or small holes, patch them up with a bit of raw pastry pressed over. Using a fork, prick the bottom of the pastry case all over. Put the case back in the oven for 5–10 minutes, to cook and crisp up the bottom.

9. Now your pastry case is blind-baked and ready for your chosen filling. If you like, you can trim it so the edges are perfect, using a sharp, serrated knife.

TIP
You can make the pastry dough up to a day in advance and keep it wrapped and resting in the fridge. You can also freeze it for up to a month.

TIP
When making pastry it's essential to keep everything as cold as possible. If you think things are getting a little warm, stop at whatever stage you're at, pop everything in the fridge for 5 minutes and run your hands under cold water, then begin again.

TIP
You can use any dried beans, such as cannellini and flageolet, for blind-baking. You can also use dry rice. I have a mixture of rice and beans stored in a tin that I use over and over again and have had for years.

White bread dough

◆◆◆

This is a white bread dough I've used for years. It's pretty basic but yields a wonderful dough. To make a loaf, turn to the recipe for my Northern soul stack (page 47). You could follow the same recipe to make individual rolls. I also use this dough for focaccia (page 135) and pizzas (page 136).

- 1KG/2LB 4OZ/8 CUPS STRONG WHITE BREAD FLOUR, PLUS EXTRA FOR DUSTING
- 3 TSP SEA SALT
- 650ML/23FL OZ/2¾ CUPS TEPID WATER
- 14G DRIED YEAST OR 28G FRESH YEAST
- 1 TBSP CASTER (SUPERFINE) SUGAR
- 100ML/3½FL OZ/6–7 TBSP EXTRA VIRGIN OLIVE OIL

1. Mix the flour and salt together in a large bowl. Pour the water into another bowl, add the yeast, sugar and oil and stir. Leave for a couple of minutes to activate the yeast; you'll know when this has happened as there will be bubbles in the mixture.

2. Slowly pour the wet ingredients over the dry and mix to form a sticky dough. Turn out onto a floured surface and knead the dough for 10 minutes, adding a little extra flour if you need it. Set a timer, because 10 minutes is longer than you think when kneading bread!

3. Pop the dough into a lightly oiled bowl and cover with a clean tea towel. Leave in a warm place for an hour to rise.

4. The dough will have doubled in size. You now need to knock it back. Remove the tea towel and punch the dough to knock out the air. It can be used immediately for some recipes, while for others it will need to rise a second time.

TIP
When making bread, the water needs to be warm enough to activate the yeast but not so hot that the yeast cells are killed. I usually start with boiling water and add cold water to make up the total amount: roughly two-thirds boiling to one-third cold. So, for this recipe I'd use 400ml/14fl oz boiling water plus 250ml/9fl oz cold water.

◆◆◆◆◆◆◆◆◆◆◆◆◆◆◆◆◆◆◆◆◆

New Year, New Baking Rules

◆◆◆◆◆◆◆◆◆◆◆◆◆◆◆◆◆◆◆◆◆

◆◆◆◆◆◆◆◆◆◆◆◆◆◆◆◆◆◆◆◆◆◆◆◆◆◆◆

January is a time to unwind and recoup
after the busy Christmas period. But just because we
take our foot off the pedal doesn't mean we aren't
thinking about delicious, indulgent desserts.
Winter baking typically consists of lots of pastry and
heavy desserts, often laden with custard. When I was
growing up I had a pudding like this every night. It's
traditional where I'm from to eat this 'fill-you-up' food
on a daily basis, nodding back to the days when feeding
the family meant supplying enough calories to keep
them going. If, like me, you don't feel a meal's
complete without something sweet, but don't want
to indulge too heavily, you'll love this section.
This isn't all about low fat; there are also
a couple of gluten-free desserts to show that giving
up wheat need not be as difficult as you might imagine.
So this chapter is simply me saying, 'You want a dessert
that's not too naughty? This is the place for you!'

◆◆◆◆◆◆◆◆◆◆◆◆◆◆◆◆◆◆◆◆◆◆◆◆◆◆◆

Skinny carrot meringue cake

◆◆

Fancy a cake that contains no butter? Then this is the one for you. Even the meringue frosting is fat-free. This cake dates back to medieval times, when sugar was scarce and carrots (which contain lots of natural sweetness) were used instead. I eat this throughout the year, not just when I'm watching the calories; it's that good.

MAKES 1 X 20CM/8IN ROUND CAKE

- ◆ 200ML/7FL OZ VEGETABLE OIL, PLUS EXTRA FOR GREASING
- ◆ 3 EGGS
- ◆ 300G/10½OZ/1½ CUPS SOFT LIGHT BROWN SUGAR
- ◆ 600G/1LB 5OZ CARROTS, SCRUBBED AND GRATED
- ◆ 280G/10OZ/2¼ CUPS SELF-RAISING FLOUR
- ◆ 1 TSP BICARBONATE OF SODA (BAKING SODA)
- ◆ 1 TSP GROUND CINNAMON
- ◆ 1 TSP MIXED SPICE (PUMPKIN PIE SPICE)
- ◆ FINELY GRATED ZEST OF 1 ORANGE
- ◆ 150G/5½OZ/SCANT 1 CUP DRIED FRUITS, SUCH AS CHERRIES, SULTANAS (GOLDEN RAISINS), RAISINS (OPTIONAL)
- ◆ 150G/5½OZ/1¼ CUPS NUTS, SUCH AS PECANS OR WALNUTS, TOASTED AND ROUGHLY CHOPPED
- ◆ ORANGE-BLOSSOM HONEY, TO SERVE

MERINGUE FROSTING

- ◆ 6 EGG WHITES
- ◆ 300G/10½OZ/1½ CUPS CASTER (SUPERFINE) SUGAR
- ◆ 1 TSP VANILLA EXTRACT

1. Preheat the oven to 180°C/350°F/gas mark 4. Grease 2 x 20cm/8in diameter cake tins and line with baking parchment.

2. Put the oil, eggs and sugar into a bowl and beat together. Add the carrots and beat until incorporated.

3. Sift the flour, bicarbonate of soda and spices into a large bowl. Add the orange zest, dried fruits and nuts and stir to coat them in the flour; this will prevent them from sinking in the cake.

4. Add the flour mixture to the carrot mixture in 3 batches, stirring gently after each addition. Divide the mixture between the prepared tins and bake for 40 minutes, or until a skewer comes out clean. Leave to cool in the tins for 10 minutes, then turn out onto a wire rack and leave to cool completely.

5. To make the frosting, place a large heatproof bowl over a pan of simmering water, making sure the bottom of the bowl doesn't touch the water. Add the egg whites and sugar and beat with an electric hand whisk until stiff peaks form; this should take about 6 minutes. Remove from the heat, add the vanilla and give it a final few seconds beating. Your frosting will be thick and shiny and must be used right away.

6. Place the first cake on a cake board or plate and spread over the meringue frosting – not too much, or it will be pushed out of the sides. Stack the next cake layer on top. Now cover the outside of the cake; I use a palette knife and swipe the frosting up and around the sides, and I think this cake looks better when the frosting isn't smooth. If you're feeling really adventurous, blast the top gently with a blowtorch for a toasted marshmallow effect. Drizzle with a little honey to serve. The cake keeps in an airtight container for up to 2 days.

Choconut torte

◆◆

Chocolate on a diet? Am I sure? Well, this no-bake torte contains no butter, sugar, eggs or flour, and you won't believe how creamy and rich it is. And the best bit is it takes just 20 minutes to make. The avocados add a beautiful creaminess, and I promise that you can't detect their taste. Tried and tested by the whole McClements family of Sunderland.

MAKES 1 X 20CM/8IN CAKE

HAZELNUT BASE

◆ 200G/7OZ/1½ CUPS HAZELNUTS, TOASTED
◆ 25G/1OZ COCOA POWDER
◆ 75ML/5 TBSP MAPLE SYRUP
◆ 1 TBSP VEGETABLE OIL

CHOCOLATE MOUSSE TOPPING

◆ 200G/7OZ DARK CHOCOLATE (70% COCOA SOLIDS), BROKEN INTO PIECES
◆ 3 RIPE AVOCADOS, FLESH SCOOPED OUT
◆ 150ML/5FL OZ/½ CUP MAPLE SYRUP
◆ 2 TBSP PEANUT BUTTER
◆ 25G/1OZ COCOA POWDER

1. Line a 20cm/8in round or square cake tin with baking parchment.

2. For the base, put all the ingredients in a food processor and blitz until combined. Press the mixture firmly into the prepared tin, smoothing it out with the back of a spoon. Cover and place in the fridge.

3. For the mousse, put the chocolate in a heatproof bowl and melt over a pan of simmering water, making sure the bottom of the bowl does not touch the water. Put the avocado flesh, maple syrup, peanut butter and cocoa in a food processor and blend until smooth. Add the melted chocolate and blend again.

4. Pour the mousse over the base, cover and chill. If you prefer the mousse a little softer, take it out of the fridge 30 minutes before you eat it. Keep the torte in the fridge for up to 5 days.

Honey madeleines

These little French cakes are unbelievably light and moreish, and I love to serve them with poached fruits. A very small amount of butter goes into making a large batch of madeleines, so I always find them lighter than a sponge cake. Please experiment with flavours: the possibilities are endless. Try rose-water instead of honey, and lightly ground toasted pistachios instead of orange zest. It's worth investing in a proper 12-hole madeleine pan with fluted moulds: they are inexpensive and make all the difference to the texture and appearance of the madeleines.

MAKES 24 MADELEINES

- 3 EGGS
- 100G/3½OZ/½ CUP CASTER (SUPERFINE) SUGAR
- 100G/3½OZ/GENEROUS ¾ CUP PLAIN (ALL-PURPOSE) FLOUR, PLUS EXTRA FOR DUSTING
- 1 TSP BAKING POWDER
- GRATED ZEST OF 1 ORANGE
- 1 TSP ORANGE-BLOSSOM RUNNY HONEY, OR REGULAR RUNNY HONEY
- 100G/3½OZ/7 TBSP UNSALTED BUTTER, MELTED, PLUS EXTRA FOR GREASING
- ICING (CONFECTIONERS') SUGAR, FOR DUSTING
- COINTREAU SYRUP, FOR DRIZZLING (PAGE 32)

1. Preheat the oven to 190°C/375°F/gas mark 5. Butter a madeleine pan, then lightly dust it with flour, tapping off any excess.

2. Whisk the eggs and sugar together in a large bowl for at least 3 minutes, until light and mousse-like.

3. Sift the flour and baking powder over the mixture, add the orange zest and honey and fold them in. Add the melted butter and fold in gently. Cover and leave in the fridge for around 10 minutes to thicken.

4. Spoon 1 tbsp of the batter into the middle of each prepared mould; it will spread out as it bakes. Bake for 10 minutes, until golden. Turn out onto a wire rack to cool while you bake the next batch.

5. To serve, dust the madeleines with icing sugar and drizzle with Cointreau syrup. Eat them within 24 hours.

Mango and passion fruit roulade

A soft, chewy meringue, encasing fruits that are bursting with flavour, it's hard to believe this is low in fat and gluten-free. This was the darling of the 1970s' dinner party (when it was filled with cream). When buying passion fruit, it's important to choose the shrivelled ones: the fruits with smooth skins aren't ripe and their seeds will be bitter and unappealing. Change the soft fruits to suit the season: strawberries in the summer, perhaps pears in the winter. Chop your fruits and scatter them before rolling the roulade. Frozen fruits are perfect, too.

SERVES 6-8

- ◆ A LITTLE BUTTER, FOR GREASING
- ◆ 3 EGG WHITES
- ◆ 175G/6OZ/GENEROUS ¾ CUP CASTER (SUPERFINE) SUGAR
- ◆ 1 TSP CORNFLOUR (CORNSTARCH)
- ◆ 1 TSP VINEGAR (WHITE, CIDER OR MALT IS FINE)
- ◆ ICING (CONFECTIONERS') SUGAR, FOR DUSTING
- ◆ 150G/5½OZ/GENEROUS ½ CUP FAT-FREE NATURAL YOGURT, OR LOW-FAT, READY-MADE CUSTARD
- ◆ 1 MANGO, PEELED AND CHOPPED OR PULPED IN A BLENDER
- ◆ 1 WELL-WRINKLED PASSION FRUIT, SEEDS AND PULP SCOOPED OUT

1. Preheat the oven to 150°C/300°F/gas mark 2. Grease a 33 x 20cm/13 x 8in baking tin and line with baking parchment.

2. Put the egg whites in a large, clean bowl and beat quickly until they are frothy and white (you can use a food mixer, an electric whisk or a balloon whisk; it's important that the bowl and whisk are spotlessly clean, as egg whites won't whip up properly if there's any grease or fat present). Add the sugar in a steady stream, beating continuously, until it's all incorporated. Continue beating until the mixture is thick and shiny and forms stiff peaks; you should be able to take the beater out and hold the bowl upside-down without the mixture moving. Fold in the cornflour and vinegar. Gently spread the mixture into the prepared tin, taking care not to knock the air out. Bake for 30 minutes.

3. Remove the meringue from the oven, cover with a damp, clean tea towel and leave for about 15 minutes.

4. Dust a piece of greaseproof paper (wax paper) with icing sugar and turn the cooked meringue out onto the sugar, peeling back the lining paper.

5. Spread the yogurt or custard over the roulade and scatter the prepared mango and passion fruit all over the top. Roll up the roulade as tightly as you can, using the greaseproof paper it is lying on to help you. Approach it with confidence and it won't break. Dust with icing sugar and serve. If you don't finish it you can keep it in the fridge for up to 5 days.

Brown Betty baked peaches with amaretti cream

My Auntie Josephine makes an amazing crumble-type dessert with breadcrumbs and brown sugar, which she calls a Brown Betty. I've left the breadcrumbs out to make the dish lighter and it works just as well. Baking the fruit intensifies its flavour, and the richness of the amaretti cream cuts through the sweetness of the peaches while adding flavour and texture. If you aren't watching your calorie intake, whack a scoop of the best vanilla ice cream on the side of the plate and drizzle the lot with honey.

SERVES 4

◆ 4 PEACHES
◆ 1 VANILLA POD (OPTIONAL BUT TASTY)
◆ 150ML/5FL OZ/⅔ CUP SWEET WINE, SUCH AS MARSALA
◆ 4 TSP SOFT LIGHT BROWN SUGAR

AMARETTI CREAM

◆ 8 AMARETTI BISCUITS
◆ 8 TBSP FAT-FREE NATURAL FROMAGE FRAIS OR RICOTTA
◆ 1 TSP HONEY (OPTIONAL)

1. Preheat the oven to 180°C/350°F/gas mark 4.

2. Cut the peaches in half and remove the stones. (I prefer to keep the skins on, but if you like, peel the peaches by dropping them in boiling water for a minute, then draining them; the skin will slide off.)

3. Place the peaches in an ovenproof dish. Slit the vanilla pod lengthwise, scrape out the seeds and add them to a measuring jug with the sweet wine. Give it a stir. Pour the wine over the peaches and sprinkle the sugar over. Bake for 35 minutes, uncovered.

4. To make the amaretti cream, smash the amaretti into a bowl and mix with the fromage frais. If you like, you can sweeten to taste with the honey.

5. Fill the cavities of the peaches with the amaretti cream and serve immediately.

BAKE AHEAD
If you want to cook this up to a day ahead, put the baked peaches and their juices into a bowl and chill. Reheat at 150°C/300°F/gas mark 2 for 15–20 minutes, or ping them in a microwave at medium power for a minute or so. Make the amaretti cream while the peaches are reheating.

Gluten-free orange and almond cake

◆◆◆

I was recently asked to make a gluten-free cake for a friend and was given creative freedom on the flavour. Gluten-free flour is available from most supermarkets. This combination works well, as the ground almonds bind the cake. It's also a cracker for Christmas (excuse the bad pun). It's moist, delicious and really quick to make, takes no maturing and is as much of a showstopper as any fruit cake. For special occasions I love it with billowing whipped cream spiked with Cointreau. But it's delicious served with low-fat Greek-style yogurt, too.

MAKES 1 X 20CM/8IN ROUND CAKE

- 225G/8OZ/1 CUP UNSALTED BUTTER, AT ROOM TEMPERATURE, PLUS EXTRA FOR GREASING
- 225G/8OZ/GENEROUS 1 CUP CASTER (SUPERFINE) SUGAR
- 4 EGGS
- 50G/1¾OZ/⅓ CUP GLUTEN-FREE PLAIN FLOUR, SIFTED
- 1 TSP GLUTEN-FREE BAKING POWDER
- 225G/8OZ/2¼ CUPS GROUND ALMONDS
- GRATED ZEST AND JUICE OF 2 ORANGES
- 2 TBSP MARMALADE (USE ORANGE, LEMON, GINGER, WHATEVER YOU LIKE)
- 2 TBSP DEMERARA SUGAR
- SMALL HANDFUL OF TOASTED SLIVERED ALMONDS, TO DECORATE
- LOW-FAT, GREEK-STYLE YOGURT, TO SERVE

1. Preheat the oven to 200°C/400°F/gas mark 6. Grease a 20cm/8in diameter cake tin and line it with baking parchment.

2. Beat the butter for a minute or so, until light and fluffy. Add the sugar and beat until incorporated. Scrape down the bowl to ensure all the ingredients are combined. Beat in the eggs one at a time, adding a tablespoon of the flour after each egg to keep the mixture smooth.

3. Mix the rest of the flour and the baking powder with the almonds, then stir in the orange zest.

4. Slowly add the flour mixture to the butter and egg mixture, beating. Scrape down the bowl to ensure everything is evenly mixed, then fold in the orange juice. Spoon into the prepared tin and level the top of the batter.

5. Drop half-teaspoons of marmalade all over the surface (you don't have to cover the top or spread it out; just dollop it on). Sprinkle with the demerara sugar and bake for 35–45 minutes, or until a knife or skewer comes out clean. Leave to cool slightly. Just before serving, scatter with the toasted flaked almonds. Serve with low-fat Greek-style yogurt.

COINTREAU SYRUP

If you want to turn up the volume, melt some soft brown sugar and water with some Cointreau in a pan – a few tablespoons of each, or however much you think your guests will crave. Once the sugar has dissolved, pour the syrup over the warm cake or serve it on the side for your guests to drizzle as they are eating.

Old-school gluten-free Bakewell tart

One of the first things I mastered in the kitchen was pastry and the art of blind baking. The simple and cheap ingredients that go into pastry meant that pies and tarts were a family staple for us. For me, the humble Bakewell tart is the finest of them all. If you want to go really old school, decorate it with glacé (candied) cherries. The origins of this traditional British pudding are fiercely contested, as is the name itself: is it Bakewell tart or Bakewell pudding? I say who cares? As long as you have a massive slice with a cup of tea.

MAKES 1 X 23CM/9IN TART

- 1 X 23CM/9IN BLIND-BAKED SWEET PASTRY CASE (PAGE 17; SUBSTITUTE GLUTEN-FREE PLAIN FLOUR FOR THE PLAIN (ALL-PURPOSE) FLOUR)
- 100G/3½OZ/7 TBSP UNSALTED BUTTER
- 100G/3½OZ/½ CUP CASTER (SUPERFINE) SUGAR
- 3 EGGS, PLUS 1 EGG YOLK
- 100G/3½OZ/1 CUP GROUND ALMONDS
- 1 TSP VANILLA EXTRACT
- 1 TSP ALMOND EXTRACT
- 4 TBSP YOUR FAVOURITE JAM
- 50G/1¾OZ/½ CUP SLIVERED ALMONDS

1. Prepare the filling while the pastry case is baking. Melt the butter in a pan over a medium heat and cook until it's light brown and smells nutty. Leave to cool.

2. In a large bowl, whisk together the sugar, eggs, egg yolk, almonds, vanilla extract and almond extract for a good few minutes, until light and mousse-like. Slowly pour in the cooled melted butter, whisking as you go.

3. Once the pastry case is cooked, take it out of the oven and turn the oven down to 180°C/350°F/gas mark 4.

4. Spread the jam over the bottom of the hot pastry case, then fill the case with the whisked mixture. Bake for 15 minutes, then scatter over the flaked almonds and bake for another 15–25 minutes. When it's done the top will be just firm and golden, with beautiful burnished-gold almonds. Leave to cool before serving. Keep the tart in an airtight container for up to 4 days.

Apple strudel parcels

Thank you, Austria, for Arnold Schwarzenegger and the strudel. This Viennese classic is my favourite fruit-based dessert. Traditionally it includes breadcrumbs, but I think they make the filling heavy. I grate my apples, but you can chunky-chop them if you prefer. Serve with a low-fat yogurt for dipping.

MAKES ABOUT 10 PARCELS

- 50G/1¾OZ/5 TBSP CURRANTS
- 2 TBSP BRANDY (OPTIONAL)
- A LITTLE PLAIN (ALL-PURPOSE) FLOUR, FOR DUSTING
- 4 DESSERT APPLES, SUCH AS COX, RUSSET, PINK LADY OR GRANNY SMITH
- 4 BAKING APPLES
- GRATED ZEST AND JUICE OF 1 UNWAXED LEMON
- 50G/1¾OZ/¼ CUP SOFT LIGHT BROWN SUGAR
- 50G/1¾OZ/½ CUP TOASTED SLIVERED ALMONDS
- ½ TSP GROUND CINNAMON
- ½ TSP GRATED NUTMEG
- ½ TSP MIXED SPICE (APPLE PIE SPICE)
- 1 X 275G PACK OF FILO PASTRY
- 50G/1¾OZ/4 TBSP UNSALTED BUTTER, MELTED
- 2–3 TSP DEMERARA SUGAR
- ICING (CONFECTIONERS') SUGAR, FOR DUSTING

1. If you like, soak the currants in the brandy overnight; it gives them much more flavour. Preheat the oven to 200°C/400°F/gas mark 6. Lightly flour a large baking sheet.

2. Core the apples and grate them coarsely, leaving the skins on. Once they are all grated, pat them with kitchen towel to remove some of the moisture. Toss them in the lemon juice to prevent them from discolouring, then add the light brown sugar, currants (and the brandy, if using), almonds and spices.

3. Take one sheet of filo pastry, cut it in half lengthwise and lightly brush all over with melted butter. Add a good tablespoon of the apple mixture to one end of the pastry and fold the corner up over the mixture to make a triangle. Now fold the triangle up and over itself to seal the open side. Keep turning the triangle until the filling is sealed in on all three sides. Trim off any excess filo to make a neat triangle. If the pastry doesn't stick, brush with a little more melted butter. Brush the completed triangular parcel with butter and place it on the floured baking sheet while you assemble the rest of the parcels.

4. When you've made all the parcels, sprinkle lightly with demerara sugar for added crunch. Bake for 20 minutes, until golden. Dust with icing sugar and serve warm or cold.

Breakfast Like a Queen

I know it's a cliché, but breakfast really is the most important meal of the day. In medieval England, kings and their courts enjoyed six-hour breakfasts featuring dishes such as roasted stuffed swans, pies and jelly. A bit much for a morning before hopping on the bus to work. I'm a muesli girl myself (I know, how disappointing: a baker who doesn't eat croissants...).
The aromas of baking at dawn conjure up memories of Nana Jean's kitchen on a Saturday, although bizarrely we often used to eat Scotch eggs for breakfast, not pastries.

◆◆◆◆◆◆◆◆◆◆◆◆◆◆◆◆◆◆◆◆◆

Mega fuel mash-up muesli

◆◆◆

A recipe from over 100 years ago and still tasting good. Muesli was developed by a Swiss physician to offer his convalescent patients a breakfast that is high in fibre and vitamins. I've taken the best bits of the original recipe and put my modern spin on it. Delicious, and much cheaper than buying boxed muesli from the supermarket, this can be made in bulk, so you don't have to prepare it every day. Store it in sealable plastic (Tupperware) containers for your very own homemade cereal.

**MAKES ENOUGH FOR
1 PERSON FOR SEVERAL DAYS**

- 500G/1LB 2OZ/6¼ CUPS ROLLED OATS
- 85G/3OZ/1⅓ CUPS WHEAT BRAN
- 2 HANDFULS OF MIXED NUTS, TOASTED AND CHOPPED
- 2 HANDFULS OF MIXED DRIED FRUITS (SUCH AS RAISINS, CHOPPED APRICOTS OR DATES)

TO SERVE
- 1 APPLE, GRATED
- A GOOD SPLASH OF MILK
- HANDFUL OF FRESH FRUITS (SLICED BANANA, BLUEBERRIES AND RASPBERRIES ARE MY FAVOURITES)
- 2 TSP HONEY
- 2 TSP PLAIN YOGURT

1. Put the oats, bran and your chosen nuts and dried fruits in a resealable plastic container and shake to mix. It'll keep for around 8 weeks.

2. To serve, give the container a shake before you scoop out the muesli, so everything is evenly mixed. Put a handful of the dry mixture in your cereal bowl. Mix the grated apple through the muesli. Pour over the milk and leave to soak while you prepare the fresh fruits.

3. Tumble the fruit over your moist muesli and top with the honey and yogurt. Stir, or leave it all plonked on top.

Beehive bars

On a Sunday I have two rituals: a Sunday lunch, no matter where, no matter how, and 20 minutes in the kitchen to knock up a batch of these for my breakfast through the week. The Beehive bar is a glorified flapjack packed with fruit, nuts and chocolate chips. You can leave the chocolate chips out if you like, but life's too short to worry about chocolate at breakfast!

MAKES ABOUT 16 BARS

- 225G/8OZ/1 CUP UNSALTED BUTTER, PLUS EXTRA FOR GREASING
- 225G/8OZ/GENEROUS 1 CUP SOFT LIGHT BROWN SUGAR
- 150G/5½OZ/½ CUP GOLDEN SYRUP (LIGHT CORN SYRUP)
- 450G/1LB/5½ CUPS ROLLED OATS
- SMALL HANDFUL OF MIXED NUTS (SUCH AS PISTACHIOS, HAZELNUTS, ALMONDS AND WALNUTS)
- SMALL HANDFUL OF DRIED FRUITS (SUCH AS CRANBERRIES, CURRANTS, OR CHOPPED DATES OR FIGS)
- SMALL HANDFUL OF CHOCOLATE CHIPS (WHITE, MILK OR DARK)

1. Preheat the oven to 150°C/300°F/gas mark 2. Lightly grease a loose-bottomed 33 x 20cm/13 x 8in tin or disposable foil container.

2. Melt the butter in a large saucepan. Add the sugar and golden syrup and stir until it has dissolved and everything is incorporated. Stir in the oats: you might think the mixture won't cover them all, but keep stirring and eventually they will be coated.

3. Press the mixture into the tin, then scatter with the nuts, fruits and chocolate chips, pressing them into the oats. Bake for 25 minutes. The mixture will still look quite wet and loose, but don't worry: it'll firm up as it cools.

4. Leave to cool in the tin. Once completely cold, turn out and slice into chunky bars. Keep the bars in an airtight container for up to a week and enjoy one or two of these every morning on the way to work.

WEIGHING GOLDEN SYRUP
The easy way to weigh golden syrup is to put the pan or bowl you're using on your kitchen scales and add the syrup directly into it. It doesn't matter if you're adding it to other ingredients, especially if you reset your scales to zero first.

CHOCOLATE CHIPS
Whether you prefer white, milk or dark chocolate, it's important you use chocolate chips – don't just smash up a chocolate bar. Chocolate chips are made with a stabilizer so they keep their shape and don't melt, which is what you want for these bars.

Croissants and pains au chocolat

A homemade croissant on a Sunday morning with an espresso and the papers is such a treat. Pain au chocolat is the same dough, filled with chocolate. These French breakfast classics are a lot simpler to make at home than you might think. I find croissant dough similar to the rough puff pastry that my nana taught me to make. I'm not going to lie: both are a labour of love, and there's lots of waiting time, but nothing beats a freshly baked all-butter croissant.

MAKES 12 CROISSANTS OR 12 PAINS AU CHOCOLAT

- 500G/1LB 2OZ/4 CUPS PLAIN (ALL-PURPOSE) FLOUR, PLUS EXTRA FOR DUSTING
- 10G SEA SALT
- 1 VITAMIN C TABLET, GROUND (A TIP FROM A FRENCH BAKER)
- 15G FRESH YEAST
- 50G/1¾OZ/¼ CUP CASTER (SUPERFINE) SUGAR
- 150ML/5FL OZ/⅔ CUP TEPID WHOLE MILK, MIXED WITH 150ML/5FL OZ/ ⅔ CUP TEPID WATER
- 300G/10½OZ/1¼ CUPS UNSALTED BUTTER, VERY COLD, CUT INTO CUBES
- 1 EGG, BEATEN

FOR PAINS AU CHOCOLAT

- 100G/3½OZ DARK CHOCOLATE (70% COCOA SOLIDS), ROUGHLY CHOPPED

1. You'll need to start making these the day before you intend to eat them. Sift the flour into a large mixing bowl and add the salt and a tiny pinch of the vitamin C powder, making sure it's evenly mixed through. Using your fingertips, rub in the yeast and sugar. Once they're finely crumbled and well mixed in, make a well in the centre and gradually stir in the warm milk and water. Don't overmix, just bind the dough together, using your hands. Put the dough in a plastic bag and leave it in the fridge for 6 hours or overnight.

2. On a lightly floured surface, roll out the dough into a rectangle. Dot with one-third of the cold butter, fold the dough in half so the butter is inside and roll it out again. Repeat this process, then wrap the dough in cling film (plastic wrap) and put it back in the fridge for 20 minutes.

3. Repeat the process once more, using the remaining cold butter. After you have dotted and folded (but not rolled out) for the third time, put the dough back in the fridge for 20 minutes.

4. Preheat the oven to its lowest setting. Roll out the dough into a rectangle and cut out 12 triangles if you're making croissants or 12 rectangles for pains au chocolat.

5. To make the croissants, lightly stretch the dough and roll from the long edge up to the tip of the triangle. For the pains au chocolat, add a few pieces of chopped chocolate along one of the wider sides and begin to roll them up, adding more chocolate as you go; turn the dough to make sure the joins are underneath. Put the pastries on a baking sheet, spacing them well apart as they will double in size. Brush the tops lightly with beaten egg, put the baking sheet in the oven and turn it off, so you are using the residual heat. Leave for 1 hour to rise.

6. Remove the baking sheet from the oven and turn the oven up to 200°C/400°F/gas mark 6. Brush the dough lightly with beaten egg, then bake for 10–15 minutes, until golden. Best eaten warm from the oven or at least the day they're baked.

My Northern soul stack

When I first started dancing and attending all-nighters I used to leave the club around 7am. Bearing in mind I'd probably spent the last 10 hours on the dance floor, the first thing I wanted to do was refuel my body before the long journey home, but at that time of the morning in small northern cities I would be lucky if I could find a bottle of milk, let alone a substantial meal, so I started to take my own food. One day I had some leftover bread and I made a sandwich/pie concoction from whatever my mam had in her fridge. I remember ham, pastrami, cheese and gherkins. You can imagine that after not eating for hours the sight of it emerging from my bag was music to my rumbling tummy and to my fellow Soulies. Now it's kind of a running joke – who's going to get a slice? I'm a sharer, of course – as long as I get two slices! Elvis did something similar, scooping out loaves and filling them with bananas, chocolate and peanut butter. Sounds delish, doesn't it? For all you non-Soulies out there, try this at your next picnic or on a journey when there's a few of you travelling.

SERVES 10–15

- WHITE BREAD DOUGH (PAGE 19)
- PLAIN (ALL-PURPOSE) FLOUR, FOR DUSTING

FILLING

- YOUR FAVOURITE COOKED MEATS, CHEESES AND PICKLES – AND LOADS OF THEM!

1. Shape the knocked-back bread dough and let it rise for a second time. You can bake it in a lightly oiled 900g/2lb loaf tin or you can make a big round cob loaf, which I prefer.

2. Slash the top of the dough or snip it, dust lightly with flour and cover with a clean tea towel. Leave in a warm place for 1 hour to rise, until almost doubled in size.

3. Preheat the oven to its highest setting. Carefully remove the tea towel from the dough and put the risen bread in the hot oven. For a good crust, spray water inside the oven as you put it in: the steam develops the crust of the bread. Immediately turn the oven down to 200°C/400°F/gas mark 6 and cook for 35 minutes. When it's cooked, your bread will sound hollow when tapped underneath; if you've made it in a tin, tip it out to check.

4. Cool on a wire rack so that the bottom doesn't get soggy. Leave until cold.

5. To make the stack, slice the top off the cold bread, scoop out most of the bread and layer the cavity with your chosen fillings, packing them in tight. Put the top back on and wrap tightly in cling film to secure the filling. If I've used a lot of cheese I sometimes wrap the stack in foil and pop it in the oven to melt the cheese, which acts like a glue, binding everything together. To serve, cut into very thick slices.

English muffins

This is the great British breakfast muffin, which would traditionally have been split and filled with butter and bacon or served with top-notch preserves. These muffins also make a fab sandwich, and if they start to go a little stale just toast them. We took turns to fry our own when we were younger, standing on a little step to see into my Nana Jean's frying pan. She used lard, but you could use vegetable oil instead.

MAKES 6 MUFFINS

- 225ML/8FL OZ/SCANT 1 CUP MILK
- 1 TSP CASTER (SUPERFINE) SUGAR OR HONEY
- 2 TSP DRIED YEAST
- 425G/15OZ/SCANT 3½ CUPS PLAIN (ALL-PURPOSE) FLOUR, PLUS EXTRA FOR DUSTING
- PINCH OF SALT
- LARD OR VEGETABLE OIL, FOR FRYING

1. Put the milk in a pan with 4 tbsp water and warm slightly. Remove from the heat, add the sugar or honey and the yeast, stir and then cover and leave in a draught-free place for 10 minutes.

2. Sift the flour into a large bowl, add the salt, make a well in the centre and pour in the milk-and-yeast mixture. Mix to form a non-sticky dough; you might need a little more milk – cold is fine. If the dough is too wet, add a little more flour. Turn the dough out onto a lightly floured surface and knead it for 10 minutes; set a timer, because 10 minutes is always longer than you think.

3. Put the dough back in the bowl, cover with a clean tea towel and leave in a warm place for 1 hour, until doubled in size. Tip the dough out onto a floured surface, roll out to around 1cm/½in thick and cut out 7.5cm/3in rounds. Place on a baking sheet, cover with the tea towel and leave to rise again for 30 minutes.

4. Add a little lard to a frying pan over a low heat. Once hot, add a few muffins, and cook for 5–7 minutes on each side. These are truly amazing served warm, straight out of the pan.

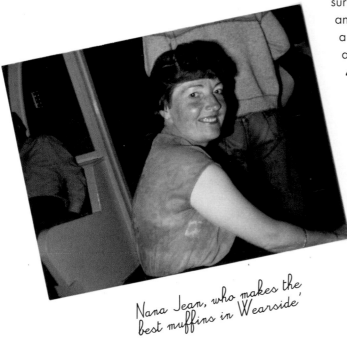

Nana Jean, who makes the best muffins in Wearside'

Lemon poppy seed muffins

One of my pet hates is a muffin that turns out flat and level. A muffin should be risen and billowing, with a distinctive 'muffin top' (cake hanging over the sides of the case). It took me a while to perfect this recipe, and I think it's foolproof. Variations are almost limitless: the classic blueberry, chocolate chip, apple strudel (made with diced apple, currants and spices), and so on. I love fresh, zingy flavours in the morning, so this variation is perfect with my espresso.

MAKES 6 LARGE MUFFINS

- 1 EGG, BEATEN
- 125ML/4FL OZ/½ CUP VEGETABLE OIL
- 115G/4OZ/GENEROUS ½ CUP CASTER (SUPERFINE) SUGAR
- 175ML/6FL OZ/¾ CUP MILK
- 250G/9OZ/2 CUPS PLAIN (ALL-PURPOSE) FLOUR
- 3 TSP BAKING POWDER
- 2 TSP POPPY SEEDS
- GRATED ZEST OF 2 UNWAXED LEMONS AND JUICE OF 4
- 2 TBSP LEMON CURD
- 2 TBSP ICING (CONFECTIONERS') SUGAR

1. Preheat the oven to 200°C/400°F/gas mark 6. Line a non-stick muffin tin with large paper muffin cases. (It's important it's non-stick, as the batter will rise and overflow outside the cases.)

2. Put the egg, oil, sugar and milk in a bowl or a food mixer with a paddle attachment. Whisk for a minute or o, until the sugar has dissolved. Sift the flour and baking powder into a bowl, then stir in the poppy seeds and lemon zest.

3. Add the flour mixture to the egg mixture and roughly mix together for a few seconds – it should remain lumpy. Fill the muffin cases almost full and top each muffin with ½ tsp lemon curd. Bake for 25 minutes, until well risen and springy to the touch. Leave to cool in the tin for a few minutes, then transfer to a wire rack and leave to cool completely.

4. To make the topping, put the icing sugar in a small bowl and add enough lemon juice to make a runny icing.

5. When the muffins are cool, dip the tops in the icing to coat the whole muffin top. Let them stand for about 10 minutes so the topping sets, then dive in. They will keep in an airtight container for 2 days.

Breakfast-in-bed banana bread

◆◆◆

Oh, how I love this weekend treat! I eat it slightly warmed in – dare I say it? – the microwave, then smothered in honey with a bit of yogurt on the side. Cake for breakfast? You might be thinking I've gone mad, but this really works, and the French have their croissants, after all. It's important you get the blackest, most overripe bananas you can for this, as they are sweet rather than starchy. If your bananas aren't ripe, this won't work.

MAKES 1 X 900 G/2 LB LOAF

- 75G/2¾OZ/GENEROUS ½ CUP WALNUTS, CHOPPED
- 2 TSP RUNNY HONEY
- 125G/4½OZ/GENEROUS ½ CUP UNSALTED BUTTER, AT ROOM TEMPERATURE, PLUS EXTRA FOR GREASING
- 175G/6OZ/GENEROUS ¾ CUP SOFT LIGHT BROWN SUGAR
- 2 EGGS
- 280G/10OZ/2¼ CUPS PLAIN (ALL-PURPOSE) FLOUR, PLUS EXTRA FOR DUSTING
- 1 TSP BICARBONATE OF SODA (BAKING SODA)
- 1 TSP VANILLA EXTRACT
- 125ML/4FL OZ/½ CUP MILK
- 4 MEDIUM RIPE BANANAS, MASHED

1. Toast the walnuts in a hot, dry pan over a medium heat for about 5 minutes, then remove from the heat, toss with the honey and set aside until needed.

2. Preheat the oven to 180°C/350°F/gas mark 4. Grease a 900g/2lb loaf tin and dust with flour, tapping out any excess; this will prevent the loaf from sticking.

3. Beat the butter for a minute or so, until light and fluffy. Add the sugar and beat until incorporated. Scrape down the bowl to ensure all the ingredients are combined. Beat in the eggs, one at a time.

4. Sift the flour together with the bicarbonate of soda. Add the vanilla to the milk.

5. Slowly add the flour mixture to the butter-and-egg mixture, alternating with the milk. Scrape down the bowl to ensure everything is evenly mixed, then fold in the bananas and honeyed walnuts. Spoon into the prepared tin and level the top of the batter.

6. Bake for 45 minutes to 1 hour, or until a skewer comes out clean. Cool in the tin on a wire rack for 10 minutes, then remove from the tin; you might need to slide a knife around it first. Store in an airtight container for up to a week. Serve generous slices with strong coffee, the newspapers and morning TV, pure bliss.

Valentine's Day

◆◆◆◆◆◆◆◆◆◆◆◆◆◆◆◆◆◆◆◆◆◆◆◆

Nothing says 'I love you' like someone putting
time and thought into making something
for you. Many of the items in this section
are perfect as gifts. You can pick up little
cellophane bags and wrappings in most craft
stores or online, and old cleaned jam jars look
so pretty filled with handmade chocolates.
Decorate with personalized tags and
ribbons for the ultimate I love you!

◆◆◆◆◆◆◆◆◆◆◆◆◆◆◆◆◆◆◆◆◆◆◆◆

Salted caramel custard and chocolate cake

When I got asked to make one of these for a graduation gift, I said 'yes' without even knowing what it was. I was pretty nervous, but I love the buzz of developing a recipe 'live', in the middle of making it. I'm so glad I thought to put the gelatine in as I don't think this would set without it. If you can't get Maldon sea salt, use another good ground sea salt – table salt won't do. Shop-bought cake is fine for this, or make a Victoria sponge. You'll need a gâteau ring as you need to stack the layers up inside it. If you don't have one, use a 20cm/8in loose-bottomed tin, stack the cake inside and push it out when set.

MAKES 1 X 20CM/8IN ROUND CAKE
- 250ML/9FL OZ/1 CUP DOUBLE CREAM
- 1 TBSP CASTER (SUPERFINE) SUGAR
- 1 X 20CM/8IN BAKED VICTORIA SPONGE, SLICED HORIZONTALLY INTO THIRDS (PAGE 81)

SALTED CARAMEL CUSTARD
- 3 LEAVES OF GELATINE
- 4 EGG YOLKS
- 140G/5OZ/SCANT ¾ CUP CASTER (SUPERFINE) SUGAR
- 70G/2½OZ/5 TBSP SALTED BUTTER, COLD AND CUBED
- 2 TSP MALDON GROUND SEA SALT
- 300ML/10FL OZ/1¼ CUPS WHOLE MILK, WARMED IN A PAN

GLOSSY CHOCOLATE TOPPING
- 150G/5½OZ/¾ CUP CASTER (SUPERFINE) SUGAR
- 200G/7OZ DARK CHOCOLATE (70% COCOA SOLIDS), FINELY CHOPPED

1. Start by making the salted caramel custard. Put the gelatine in a shallow bowl of cold water for 5 minutes. Meanwhile, beat the egg yolks in a large bowl.

2. Put the sugar in a pan with 5 tbsp water, bring to the boil and cook over a medium heat until it turns a medium amber colour. Don't stir; just swirl the pan gently if you must. Once the caramel is a good colour, add the butter and salt and swirl until melted. Whisk in the warm milk (it's essential the milk is warm, otherwise the caramel might set hard). Pour this mixture over the egg yolks and whisk continuously until combined. Return to the pan and whisk over a low heat for a minute or so, until slightly thickened.

3. Scoop the gelatine out of the soaking water, squeeze out the excess water and add it to the caramel, stirring to make sure it's completely melted. Pour the custard into a bowl and leave to cool for 10 minutes. Cover with cling film and place in the fridge for 10 minutes to chill and slightly set.

4. Whip the cream with the caster sugar. Put the 20cm/8in gâteau ring over the Victoria sponge pieces to make a neat edge, then remove. Put the gâteau ring on a baking sheet and place a layer of the cake in the bottom. Top with a little of the chilled caramel custard and then some whipped cream. Repeat the process until you're at the top of the ring, finishing with a layer of cake.

5. Cover with cling film and leave in the fridge until the custard is completely set – about 2 hours.

RECIPE CONTINUES OVERLEAF

DECORATE
YOUR CAKE
I sometimes smash
up a Crunchie bar as
a decorative topping
and dust with
edible gold glitter

6. Lift the ring off the cake (I use a blowtorch on the outside of the ring to get a nice clean lift; alternatively you can wrap kitchen paper soaked in boiling water around it). If you've used a loose-bottomed tin, simply press the bottom up to release the cake.

7. To make the glossy chocolate topping, put the sugar in a pan with 150ml/5fl oz/⅔cup water and stir over a low heat until the sugar has dissolved. Bring to the boil, then boil for 2 minutes. Remove from the heat, add the chocolate and stir until smooth. Leave to cool and thicken for 10 minutes.

8. Put the cake on a wire rack over a baking sheet. Pour the topping over it and smooth down the sides with a spatula or palette knife. Keep in the fridge until ready to serve.

Nana Jean and Granda Ernie in 1981

Red velvet cake

◆◆

When making red velvet cake, it's really important to use the right red food colouring: either Sugarflair Red Extra paste or Dr Oetker Natural Red. Don't get the standard red colouring, as the cake will turn brown when you bake it. Of course, this is not just for Valentine's Day; it's a pretty cake for parties, and the mixture makes amazing cupcakes, too.

MAKES 1 X 20CM/8IN ROUND CAKE

◆ 175G/6OZ/¾ CUP UNSALTED BUTTER, AT ROOM TEMPERATURE, PLUS EXTRA FOR GREASING
◆ 450G/1LB/2¼ CUPS CASTER (SUPERFINE) SUGAR
◆ 3 EGGS, AT ROOM TEMPERATURE
◆ 3 TBSP COCOA POWDER
◆ 38ML BOTTLE DR OETKER NATURAL RED OR 1 HEAPED TSP SUGARFLAIR RED EXTRA FOOD COLOURING
◆ 1 TSP VANILLA EXTRACT
◆ 500G/1LB 2OZ/4 CUPS PLAIN (ALL-PURPOSE) FLOUR
◆ 1 TSP SALT
◆ 340ML/12FL OZ/1½ CUPS BUTTERMILK
◆ 1½ TSP BICARBONATE OF SODA (BAKING SODA)
◆ 1½ TSP CIDER VINEGAR

CREAM CHEESE FROSTING

◆ 125G/4½OZ/GENEROUS ½ CUP UNSALTED BUTTER, AT ROOM TEMPERATURE
◆ 175G/6OZ/¾ CUP FULL-FAT SOFT CHEESE
◆ 500G/1LB 2OZ/4¼ CUPS ICING (CONFECTIONERS') SUGAR

1. Preheat the oven to 180°C/350°F/gas mark 4. Grease 2 x 20cm/8in diameter cake tins and line with baking parchment.

2. Beat the butter for a minute or so, until light and fluffy. Add the sugar and beat until incorporated. Scrape down the bowl to ensure all the ingredients are combined. Beat in the eggs, one at a time. Beat in the cocoa, food colouring and vanilla extract.

3. Sift the flour and salt into a bowl, then add to the butter mixture in three stages, alternating with the buttermilk and scraping down after each addition.

4. Put the bicarbonate of soda and cider vinegar in a small bowl and whisk until it bubbles up. Add this to the cake batter and give it one last quick beat. The addition of the vinegar and bicarbonate will make the colour of the cake develop and stay red when cooked. Spoon the mixture into the tins and level the top of the batter.

5. Bake for 45 minutes to 1 hour. After 30 minutes, cover the top of the cake with foil to prevent it from browning too much. Test the cake after 45 minutes; when it is cooked, a knife or skewer inserted in the centre will come out clean. Remove the foil and leave to cool on a wire rack for around 30 minutes. Remove from the tin and leave until completely cool before decorating.

RECIPE CONTINUES OVERLEAF

RECIPE CONTINUED FROM PREVIOUS PAGE

6. To make the frosting, beat the butter until softened, then add the soft cheese and beat for a few seconds to combine. Scrape down the bowl to make sure everything is mixed, then add the icing sugar and beat again. The longer you beat, the creamier the icing will be. Set aside at room temperature until you're ready to use it. If it's a warm day, put it in the fridge but take it out 10 minutes before you want to use it.

7. To decorate the cakes, you first need to level them. Use a bread knife to slice a small section off the top and make it as flat as possible. (Keep the sliced-off section to decorate the cake.)

8. Next you have to cut each cake in half horizontally; again, use a bread knife. Now you have four layers of cake. Put the bottom layer of cake on your cake plate. Spread with the icing, making sure it's not too thick; about 1cm/½in is perfect. Repeat with all the layers.

9. Next, cover the outside of the cake with icing; I use a palette knife or a butter knife. Finally, crumble the reserved sliced-off sections of cake, and scatter the crumbs all over the top of it. The cake will keep in an airtight container for around 4 days, but it's far too beautiful to hide or keep!

Cheesecake Smartie glitter fudge brownies

◆◆◆

A box of these brownies on Valentine's Day is guaranteed to make anyone smile. Have them delivered to your one and only's workplace with some flowers for major brownie points!

MAKES 12 BROWNIES

◆ 250G/9OZ/GENEROUS 1 CUP UNSALTED BUTTER
◆ 200G/7OZ DARK CHOCOLATE (70% COCOA SOLIDS), ROUGHLY CHOPPED
◆ 75G/2¾OZ COCOA POWDER
◆ 70G/2½OZ/GENEROUS ½ CUP PLAIN (ALL-PURPOSE) FLOUR
◆ 1 TSP BAKING POWDER
◆ 350G/12OZ/1¾ CUPS CASTER (SUPERFINE) SUGAR
◆ 4 EGGS
◆ 1 TSP VANILLA EXTRACT

CHEESECAKE LAYER

◆ 100G/3½OZ/7 TBSP FULL-FAT SOFT CHEESE
◆ 100G/3½OZ/7 TBSP MASCARPONE CHEESE
◆ 50ML/3 TBSP DOUBLE CREAM
◆ 50G/1¾OZ/¼ CUP CASTER (SUPERFINE) SUGAR
◆ 1 TSP VANILLA ESSENCE

TOPPING

◆ 100G/3½OZ WHITE CHOCOLATE, ROUGHLY CHOPPED
◆ 1 TUBE OF SMARTIES (OR SMALL PACK OF M&MS), TIPPED INTO A PLASTIC BAG AND SMASHED WITH A ROLLING PIN
◆ EDIBLE GLITTER

1. Preheat the oven to 180°C/350°F/gas mark 4. Line a 33 x 20cm/13 x 8in baking tin with greaseproof paper.

2. Place a large heatproof bowl over a pan of simmering water, making sure the bottom of the bowl doesn't touch the water. Add the butter and chocolate and mix until melted and smooth (or do this in a microwave on medium power, stirring every 30 seconds).

3. In a separate bowl, sift together the cocoa, flour and baking powder, then add the sugar. Add the dry ingredients to the melted chocolate and butter mixture and stir well.

4. Beat the eggs with the vanilla extract, add to the bowl and mix until you have a silky consistency. Pour into the lined baking tin and bake for around 25 minutes, until slightly springy to the touch. The brownie will still be wobbly, which is fine – you won't be able to test it with a knife – it will firm up as it cools. Leave to cool in the tin, then turn out.

5. To make the cheesecake layer, simply beat all the ingredients together until you have the consistency of softened butter. Spread the cheesecake mixture over the cooled brownies, levelling the top with a spatula.

6. To make the topping, place a large heatproof bowl over a pan of simmering water, making sure the bottom of the bowl doesn't touch the water. Add the white chocolate and melt, using a fork to flick the chocolate all over the cheesecake. Scatter the Smarties over the white chocolate, which will help them stick. Top with any remaining white chocolate and the edible glitter. Cut into squares and serve, or box up with ribbon and coloured tissue.

Chocolate truffles

◆◆

We make hundreds of these every Valentine's Day at my bakery and sell them in little jam jars or personalized boxes. They are embarrassingly simple to make and there are so many variations.

MAKES 24 TRUFFLES

◆ 150ML/5FL OZ/⅔ CUP DOUBLE CREAM
◆ 40G/1½OZ/3 TBSP SOFT LIGHT BROWN SUGAR
◆ 150G/5½OZ DARK CHOCOLATE, FINELY CHOPPED
◆ 1 TSP VANILLA EXTRACT
◆ 4-5 TBSP COCOA POWDER, FOR COATING

VARIATIONS

ORANGE TRUFFLES

◆ GRATED ZEST OF ½ ORANGE
◆ 2 TBSP GRAND MARNIER

HAZELNUT TRUFFLES

◆ 50G/1¾OZ HAZELNUTS, TOASTED AND FINELY CHOPPED

ALMOND CRISP TRUFFLES

◆ 6 CRISP AMARETTI BISCUITS, SMASHED

COCONUT TRUFFLES

◆ 2 TBSP MALIBU (USE 25G/1OZ DESICCATED COCONUT FOR COATING, RATHER THAN COCOA)

1. Put the cream and sugar into a pan and bring to a simmer over a medium-low heat. Stir, then remove from the heat and add the chocolate and vanilla. Stir briskly until the chocolate has melted. Now stir in your variation, if using.

2. Pour the mixture into a container at least 5cm/2in deep. Cover and place in the fridge to set for a couple of hours, or preferably overnight.

3. Use a melon baller dipped into warm water to scoop balls of truffle mix, immediately drop them into a bowl of cocoa, then use your hands to form them into perfect balls before dipping them back into the cocoa.

4. The truffles can be stored in an airtight container for a week, either at room temperature or in the fridge.

Nana Jean and Granda Ernie's wedding in 1953

Toffee and banana tart

◆◆◆

I'm not the biggest banoffee pie fan, but I really wanted to include something similar in the book. I've taken different elements from my favourite baking recipes and made something I'm very happy with. It's the candy bananas at the end that swing it for me. Give your lover a slice of this on Valentine's Day and they will be yours for ever – or at least until they've finished the whole tart.

MAKES 1 X 20CM/8IN TART
BISCUIT BASE

- 150G/5½OZ/SCANT ¾ CUP UNSALTED BUTTER
- 300G/11OZ DIGESTIVE BISCUITS (GRAHAM CRACKERS), SMASHED TO FINE CRUMBS (SEE TIP)

TOFFEE FILLING

- 100G/3½OZ/7 TBSP UNSALTED BUTTER
- 50G/1¾OZ/¼ CUP CASTER (SUPERFINE) SUGAR
- 1 TBSP GOLDEN SYRUP (LIGHT CORN SYRUP)
- 400G CAN CONDENSED MILK

CHOCOLATE TOPPING

- 100G/3½OZ DARK CHOCOLATE, ROUGHLY CHOPPED
- 3 TBSP DOUBLE CREAM

CANDY BANANAS

- 50G/1¾OZ/¼ CUP CASTER (SUPERFINE) SUGAR
- 50G/1¾OZ/4 TBSP UNSALTED BUTTER
- 2 FIRM BANANAS

1. Line a 20cm/8in round loose-bottomed tin with baking parchment. To make the base, melt the butter in a pan. Add the biscuit crumbs to the butter and stir to coat. Press the mixture into the tin, cover and chill in the fridge.

2. To make the toffee layer, melt the butter, sugar and golden syrup together in a pan, bring to the boil, then add the condensed milk and turn the heat down to medium-low. Stir continuously for 15 minutes, until the toffee is a nice brown colour: if you don't keep stirring it will burn.

3. Pour the warm caramel over the chilled base, leave to cool a little, then return to the fridge to set for around 1 hour.

4. To make the chocolate topping, place a large heatproof bowl over a pan of simmering water, making sure the bottom of the bowl doesn't touch the water. Put the chocolate and cream in the bowl and melt until fudge-like. Pour over the caramel and leave in the fridge to set for 1 hour.

5. When you're ready to serve, make the candy bananas. Heat a frying pan over a medium-high heat, add the sugar and butter and swirl until caramelized. Slice the bananas into 2.5cm/1in pieces, add them to the pan and swirl to coat them in the caramel. Serve the candy bananas on the side or on top of the tart.

> **BISCUIT CRUMBS**
> Many recipes begin with a base of biscuits crushed to fine crumbs. You can do this in a food processor, or put the biscuits in a sturdy plastic bag and smash with a rolling pin. The crumbs must be fine and even – no chunks.

White chocolate and passion fruit bars

These are such fun, a grown-up kids' treat. And passion fruit on Valentine's Day is very fitting. I tried a few bases with this, using flapjacks or digestive biscuits, but the Rice Krispie base is the best.

MAKES 12 BARS

- 50G/1¾OZ/4 TBSP UNSALTED BUTTER
- 200G/7OZ/4 CUPS MINI MARSHMALLOWS
- 200G/7OZ/7 CUPS RICE KRISPIES
- 175ML/6FL OZ/¾ CUP DOUBLE CREAM
- JUICE FROM 4 PASSION FRUITS (SEE TIP)
- 300G/10½OZ WHITE CHOCOLATE, FINELY CHOPPED
- 1 SMALL PACK (ABOUT 10G/¼OZ) POPPING CANDY, TO DECORATE

1. Line the bottom of a 20cm/8in square tin with baking parchment. In a large saucepan, melt the butter over a low heat. Add the marshmallows and stir until completely melted. Remove from the heat and add the Rice Krispies, stir until well coated, then press into the lined tin.

2. Bring the cream to a simmer in a saucepan and add the passion fruit juice, reserving a few teaspoons for the top of the bars. Stir over a medium-low heat, then add the chocolate. Immediately remove from the heat and stir continuously to melt. Leave to cool slightly.

3. Pour the white chocolate mixture over the Krispie base and chill for 2–6 hours, until firm.

4. Turn out and cut into bars, using a hot knife to get a clean line. Sprinkle over the reserved passion fruit juice and scatter with popping candy. Irresistible at any time of the year.

PASSION FRUIT JUICE

To get juice from passion fruits, start with ripe, well-wrinkled fruits. Cut them in half with a sharp knife and scoop the pulp into a food processor. Blend briefly, then rub through a sieve over a small bowl to catch the juice. Discard the seeds and pith.

Auntie Jeanette's wedding; Joan's beehive rocks!

Rhubarb tarte Tatin

My friend Sharon has an allotment that yields a bountiful amount of rhubarb. After a particularly large stash and far too much rhubarb crumble I started to play around with ideas. This was my favourite: sharp pink rhubarb with light buttery pastry in a caramel sauce, divine! Don't use tinned rhubarb, it just won't do. Luckily the small, tender, pink forced rhubarb is abundant in February, perfect for this Valentine's dessert for two. A small frying pan with a metal handle is perfect if you don't have a small tarte Tatin pan.

SERVES 2

- 100G/3½OZ ALL-BUTTER PUFF PASTRY
- 3 LONG TENDER STALKS OF PINK RHUBARB
- 70G/2½OZ/⅓ CUP GRANULATED SUGAR
- 90G/3¼OZ/6 TBSP UNSALTED BUTTER, COLD AND CUBED
- GRATED ZEST OF 1 ORANGE
- SEEDS SCRAPED FROM 1 VANILLA POD
- CLOTTED CREAM OR VANILLA ICE CREAM, TO SERVE

1. If you want to make your own pastry, follow the croissant recipe (page 44) up to the end of step 2 (don't give it the final rising).

2. Whether shop-bought or homemade, roll out the pastry to around 5mm/¼in thick. Cut out a rough circle slightly larger than your pan, place it on a baking sheet, prick it all over with a fork and chill it in the fridge. Preheat the oven to 190°C/375°F/gas mark 5.

3. Cut the rhubarb into quite long pieces. You'll need two layers of rhubarb, as it can break down quite a bit.

4. Put the sugar in an ovenproof frying pan, about 15cm/6in in diameter, and put the pan over a medium-high heat. Don't stir the sugar, just swirl the pan from time to time until you have a deep-coloured caramel. Take the pan off the heat and stir in the butter, orange zest and vanilla seeds. You need to work quickly so the caramel doesn't set.

5. Arrange the rhubarb in a criss-cross pattern over the caramel, and place the pastry over the rhubarb, tucking in the sides. Bake for 25 minutes, until the pastry is puffed up and golden.

6. Carefully remove the tart from the oven and leave to settle for 2 minutes. Use a knife to release the pastry from the side of the pan. Using oven mitts, invert a serving plate over the pan and turn over; the tart should fall onto the plate. Serve warm, with a scoop of ice cream or clotted cream. One plate, two spoons.

Shortbread heart lollipops

◆◆

This is my standard shortbread recipe, passed down from generation to generation and now on to you. It's pretty simple, and is the recipe I used for dessert in the MasterChef invention test. You'll need to buy a heart cutter (not a huge investment) and some lollipop sticks, which you can get online or from craft and cake supply stores. They look pretty with ribbon tied around the sticks. A beautiful handmade gift for Valentine's Day.

MAKES 12 LOLLIPOPS

- ◆ 400G/14OZ/3¼ CUPS PLAIN (ALL-PURPOSE) FLOUR, PLUS EXTRA FOR DUSTING
- ◆ 300G/10½OZ/1¼ CUPS UNSALTED BUTTER, COLD AND CUBED, PLUS EXTRA FOR GREASING
- ◆ 150G/5½OZ/¾ CUP CASTER (SUPERFINE) SUGAR
- ◆ SEEDS SCRAPED FROM 1 VANILLA POD (OPTIONAL)

TO DECORATE

- ◆ 150G/5½OZ FONDANT ICING SUGAR
- ◆ FOOD COLOURING OF YOUR CHOICE
- ◆ SPRINKLES AND DECORATIONS OF YOUR CHOICE

1. Put the flour, butter, sugar and vanilla seeds, if using, in a bowl and either rub in with your fingertips, pulse in a food processor or combine in a food mixer. Press the mixture into a tight ball, wrap in cling film and chill for 10 minutes.

2. Preheat the oven to 190°C/375°F/gas mark 5. Lightly grease a large baking sheet. Roll out the dough on a lightly floured surface to about 1cm/½in thick (don't roll it too thin or the sticks won't go in properly; I find it easier to roll small pieces at a time). Cut out heart shapes and place them on the prepared baking sheet.

3. Press a lollipop stick gently into the point of each heart, making sure about 1cm/½in of the stick is in the shortbread so it stays in place once baked. Bake for 15 minutes. Leave to cool completely on a wire rack before handling or the sticks will come out.

4. To decorate, mix the fondant icing sugar with boiling water according to the packet instructions. Colour with food colouring if you like. Spoon over the hearts or carefully dip the front of the hearts and decorate with sugar sprinkles.

◆◆◆◆◆◆◆◆◆◆◆◆◆◆◆◆◆◆◆◆◆

Mother's Day
& Vintage Tea

◆◆◆◆◆◆◆◆◆◆◆◆◆◆◆◆◆◆◆◆◆

◆◆◆◆◆◆◆◆◆◆◆◆◆◆◆◆◆◆◆◆◆◆◆◆◆

Through the warmer months I run a vintage
tea-party service. I have a 1970s VW campervan
that I travel around in, providing tea and baked
treats with a vintage backdrop. If you want
to recreate something similar, I suggest you
root around charity shops or visit your elderly
relatives and their friends – they always have fab
vintage china and old teapots. Table decorations
can be as simple as jam jars stuffed with fresh
flowers, candles and other vintage ornaments.

◆◆◆◆◆◆◆◆◆◆◆◆◆◆◆◆◆◆◆◆◆◆◆◆◆

'The Jules' raspberry, rose and vanilla cake

◆◆

My mam, Julie, is the hardest person to buy presents for, but one thing's a dead cert – on her birthday in March there's always one of these cakes on the table. The combination of the sharp fruit and sweet syrup is to die for. Génoise sponge makes a very light cake. This is a standard Génoise batter that can be used as a building block for all kinds of cakes and pâtisserie. The Génoise needs to be made in two tins, to get the effect of the layers.

MAKES 1 X 20CM/8IN ROUND CAKE

◆ 250G/9OZ/1¼ CUPS CASTER (SUPERFINE) SUGAR
◆ 8 EGGS
◆ 100G/3½OZ/7 TBSP UNSALTED BUTTER, PLUS EXTRA FOR GREASING
◆ 250G/9OZ/2 CUPS PLAIN (ALL-PURPOSE) FLOUR
◆ SMALL HANDFUL OF PISTACHIOS, FINELY CHOPPED, TO DECORATE (OPTIONAL)

ROSE SYRUP

◆ 75G/2¾OZ/⅓ CUP CASTER (SUPERFINE) SUGAR
◆ 100ML/3½FL OZ/6–7 TBSP ROSE WATER (OR TO TASTE; LESS IF CONCENTRATED)
◆ SEEDS SCRAPED FROM 1 VANILLA POD

RASPBERRY MOUSSE

◆ 100G/3½OZ/SCANT 1 CUP RASPBERRIES, PLUS EXTRA TO DECORATE
◆ 2 TBSP ICING (CONFECTIONERS') SUGAR
◆ 250ML/9FL OZ/GENEROUS 1 CUP DOUBLE CREAM

ROSE BUTTERCREAM

◆ 115G/4OZ/½ CUP UNSALTED BUTTER, AT ROOM TEMPERATURE
◆ 1 TSP VANILLA EXTRACT
◆ 3 TBSP MILK
◆ 1 TSP ROSE WATER
◆ 500G/1LB 2OZ/4¼ CUPS ICING (CONFECTIONERS') SUGAR

1. Preheat the oven to 180°C/350°F/gas mark 4. Grease 2 x 20cm/8in tins and line with baking parchment.

2. Place a large heatproof bowl over a pan of simmering water on a medium heat, making sure the bottom of the bowl doesn't touch the water. Put the sugar and eggs in the bowl and whisk until the mixture is hot. Remove from the heat and beat for 10 minutes more, until doubled in volume, light and mousse-like.

3. Melt the butter in a pan and cook until it smells nutty and turns light brown. Leave until almost cool. Gently pour the butter into the egg mixture, whisking continuously.

4. Sift the flour and fold it into the egg mixture. Divide the mixture between the 2 tins and bake for 25 minutes, or until a skewer comes out clean. Leave to cool in the tins for a few minutes, then turn out and leave it to cool on a wire rack.

5. To make the syrup, put the sugar, rose water and vanilla seeds in a pan with 3 tbsp water, then boil for 5 minutes, until syrupy and slightly reduced. It will thicken as it cools.

6. To make the mousse, blend the raspberries with the icing sugar and pass through a sieve. Whip the cream until stiff, then fold in the raspberry purée. Cover and chill.

7. To make the buttercream, beat the butter until softened, then add the vanilla, milk, rose water and icing sugar and beat until creamy and thick.

8. To assemble, cut both cakes in half so you have 4 slices. Place one of the cakes on a board. Drizzle liberally with the rose syrup and spread with a third of the raspberry mousse. Repeat, finishing with a cake. Crumb-coat (see page 14) the cake and leave to set for 10 minutes. Spread the buttercream over the cake using a hot palette knife. Top with raspberries and pistachios, if you like.

Lemon and almond cake

The topping on this is awesome; I used to make it with just butter, sugar and almonds, but sometimes the sugar would crystalize. Liquid glucose helps prevent the formation of sugar crystals – you can buy it from supermarkets or pharmacies. The cake can be made gluten-free by replacing the self-raising flour with gluten-free self-raising flour. It is a beautifully moist tea-time cake.

MAKES 1 X 20CM/8IN ROUND CAKE

- 225G/8OZ/1 CUP UNSALTED BUTTER, AT ROOM TEMPERATURE, PLUS EXTRA FOR GREASING
- 225G/8OZ/GENEROUS 1 CUP CASTER (SUPERFINE) SUGAR
- 4 EGGS
- 100G/3½OZ/GENEROUS ¾ CUP SELF-RAISING FLOUR
- 2 TSP ALMOND EXTRACT
- 225G/8OZ/2¼ CUPS GROUND ALMONDS
- GRATED ZEST OF 2 UNWAXED LEMONS

TOPPING

- 50G/1¾OZ/4 TBSP UNSALTED BUTTER
- 50G/1¾OZ/¼ CUP SOFT LIGHT BROWN SUGAR
- 50G/1¾OZ LIQUID GLUCOSE
- 100G/3½OZ/1 CUP SLIVERED ALMONDS

1. Preheat the oven to 180°C/350°F/gas mark 4. Grease a 20cm/8in diameter tin and line with baking parchment.

2. Beat the butter for a minute or so, until light and fluffy. Add the sugar and beat until incorporated. Scrape down the bowl to ensure all the ingredients are combined. Beat in the eggs one at a time, adding 1 tbsp flour after each egg to keep the mixture smooth. Add the almond extract.

3. Sift the remaining flour and add the ground almonds and lemon zest. Slowly beat the dry ingredients into the butter-and-egg mixture – do not overbeat. Scrape down the bowl to ensure everything is evenly mixed. Spoon the mixture into the tin and level the top.

4. Bake for 35 minutes, until pale golden and just springy to the touch.

5. Meanwhile, make the topping: put the butter, sugar and glucose in a pan and melt over a low heat. Boil for 10–20 seconds, until syrupy, then add the almonds and pour over the cake.

6. Return the cake to the oven for 10 minutes. Test with a knife or skewer: if the cake is still not cooked, cover it with foil to prevent the almonds from browning too much and return to the oven for an additional 5 minutes or so.

7. Leave to cool slightly before turning out. You'll need to run a knife around the tin as the topping can be sticky. The cake will keep in an airtight container for up to 4 days.

Victoria sandwich

◆◆

A British classic, the Victoria sponge cake was named after Queen Victoria, who favoured a slice of it with her afternoon tea. Anyone who followed me on MasterChef will remember this was the huge cake I served to the board of the Women's Institute. Always use vanilla extract rather than vanilla essence.

MAKES 1 X 20CM/8IN ROUND CAKE

◆ 350G/12OZ/1½ CUPS UNSALTED BUTTER, AT ROOM TEMPERATURE, PLUS EXTRA FOR GREASING
◆ 350G/12OZ/1¾ CUPS CASTER (SUPERFINE) SUGAR
◆ 6 EGGS, BEATEN
◆ 300G/10½OZ/SCANT 2½ CUPS SELF-RAISING FLOUR
◆ 2 TSP VANILLA EXTRACT
◆ 35G/1¼OZ/¼ CUP CORNFLOUR (CORNSTARCH)

FILLING

◆ 6 TSP GOOD-QUALITY STRAWBERRY JAM
◆ 150G/5½OZ STRAWBERRIES, HULLED AND HALVED
◆ 400ML/14FL OZ/2 CUPS WHIPPING OR DOUBLE CREAM
◆ 25G/1OZ/2 TBSP CASTER (SUPERFINE) SUGAR
◆ 1 TSP VANILLA EXTRACT
◆ ICING (CONFECTIONERS') SUGAR, FOR DUSTING

1. Preheat the oven to 180°C/350°F/gas mark 4. Grease a 20cm/8in round, deep, loose-bottomed cake tin.

2. Beat the butter for a minute or so, then gradually add the sugar and beat until pale. Scrape down the bowl to ensure the ingredients are combined. Beat in the eggs a little at a time, adding 1 tbsp of the flour after each addition. Beat in the vanilla.

3. Sift the remaining flour and cornflour together, then add to the butter mixture and beat gently until just combined. Scrape down the bowl and give a final quick beat. Spoon the mixture into the prepared tin and bake for 45 minutes, until golden and springy to the touch.

4. Leave in the tin for 5 minutes, then turn out onto a wire rack to cool completely.

5. When the cake is cold, slice it in half horizontally. Place the bottom layer on a serving plate and spread the jam all over. Cover with the halved strawberries, flat-side down and cut-side out. Whip the cream with the caster sugar and vanilla extract until soft peaks form, then pipe or spoon this over the cake and cover with the top sponge. Dust with icing sugar. Eat straight away.

Mam and me with cousin Andrew

Old-school fondant fancies

◆◆◆

I was so over cupcakes the minute I gave a box of these little beauties to a friend for her birthday. They are very pretty, and because they are encased in icing they keep for a lot longer than cupcakes. They're essentially a cube of syrup-soaked sponge dipped in fondant icing. You can pick up small foil cake cases and edible flowers at most cake-supply stores or online.

MAKES 12

- 175G/6OZ/¾ CUP UNSALTED BUTTER, AT ROOM TEMERATURE, PLUS EXTRA FOR GREASING
- 175G/6OZ/GENEROUS ¾ CUP CASTER (SUPERFINE) SUGAR
- 3 EGGS
- 150G/5½OZ/1¼ CUPS SELF-RAISING FLOUR
- 15G/½OZ/2 TBSP CORNFLOUR (CORNSTARCH)
- GRATED ZEST OF 1 UNWAXED LEMON
- 1 TSP VANILLA EXTRACT

SYRUP

- 100G/3½OZ/½ CUP CASTER (SUPERFINE) SUGAR
- SEEDS SCRAPED FROM 1 VANILLA POD

TO DECORATE

- FONDANT ICING SUGAR
- FOOD COLOURING
- SPRINKLES, SUGAR FLOWERS AND EDIBLE GLITTER

1. Preheat the oven to 180°C/350°F/gas mark 4. Grease a 20cm/8in square tin and line with baking parchment.

2. Beat the butter for a minute or so, until light and fluffy. Add the sugar and beat until incorporated. Scrape down the bowl to ensure the ingredients are combined. Beat in the eggs one at a time, adding a tablespoon of the flour after each egg to keep the mixture smooth.

3. Sift the remaining flour and cornflour with the lemon zest. Slowly beat the dry ingredients into the butter and egg mixture, then add the vanilla – do not overbeat. Scrape down the bowl to ensure everything is evenly mixed. Spoon into the tin and level the top. Bake for 35 minutes, until golden and springy to the touch.

4. Meanwhile, make the syrup: put the sugar, vanilla seeds and 7 tbsp water in a pan over a low heat until the sugar dissolves. Bring to the boil and boil for 2 minutes. Set aside.

5. While the cake is still warm, slice off the top level with a bread knife. Cut the cake into 4cm/1½in cubes. Drop the cubes into the sugar syrup, then immediately lift out using a slotted spoon and place on a wire rack to allow excess syrup to drip off. Leave until completely cold.

6. To decorate, prepare the fondant icing according to the packet instructions. Add food colouring of your choice. Pour the icing over the cold, syrup-soaked cakes. It's a messy business but you will get a perfect finish if you pour loads of the icing over the sponge and allow it to drip down. (If you put some baking parchment under the wire rack you can scoop up the excess icing and re-pour.) Before the icing sets, decorate with sprinkles, sugar flowers or edible glitter – or wait for the icing to set, then use a little more fondant icing in a small piping bag to write on the cakes.

7. Put into foil or paper cases and box up, ready to present to your mam on Mother's Day.

Billionaires' shortbread

This recipe came about when I was looking for a new chocolate biscuit recipe. I knew all the components I wanted to go into it – brownie, toffee, hazelnuts and chocolate – and after a few trials the billionaires' shortbread was born. It's very rich, so it's lovely cut into small pieces, and it's easy to slice up once chilled. The middle layer is a cheat's toffee (perfect for a banoffee pie, too). It sounds like a lot of stages, but the whole process won't take any more than 2 hours – and most of that is chilling time.

MAKES ABOUT 15–20 PIECES

CHOCOLATE BASE

◆ 100G/3½OZ DARK CHOCOLATE (70% COCOA SOLIDS), ROUGHLY CHOPPED
◆ 100G/3½OZ/7 TBSP UNSALTED BUTTER
◆ 200G/7OZ/1 CUP SOFT LIGHT BROWN SUGAR
◆ 3 EGGS, BEATEN
◆ 200G/7OZ/GENEROUS 1½ CUPS SELF-RAISING FLOUR
◆ 2 TBSP COCOA POWDER

HAZELNUT TOFFEE LAYER

◆ 100G/3½OZ/7 TBSP UNSALTED BUTTER
◆ 1 TBSP GOLDEN SYRUP (LIGHT CORN SYRUP)
◆ 50G/1¾OZ/¼ CUP CASTER (SUPERFINE) SUGAR
◆ 400G CAN CONDENSED MILK
◆ 100G/3OZ/¾ CUP TOASTED HAZELNUTS, ROUGHLY CHOPPED

CHOCOLATE TOPPING

◆ 100G/3½OZ DARK CHOCOLATE (70% COCOA SOLIDS), ROUGHLY CHOPPED
◆ 1 TSP VEGETABLE OIL

1. Preheat the oven to 180°C/350°F/gas mark 4. Line a 20cm/8in square loose-bottomed tin with baking parchment (or use a 33 x 20cm/13 x 8in disposable foil container).

2. To make the chocolate base, melt the chocolate and butter together in a saucepan over a low-medium heat. Remove from the heat, stir in the sugar and then beat in the eggs. Sift the flour and cocoa together, then beat into the chocolate mixture until evenly combined. Spoon into the prepared tin and bake for 20–25 minutes. Leave in the tin on a wire rack to cool slightly; it will firm up as it cools.

3. To make the hazelnut toffee layer, melt the butter, syrup and sugar in a saucepan over a medium heat, bring to the boil, then add the condensed milk. Turn the heat to medium-low and cook, stirring continuously, for 10–15 minutes, until the mixture is a dark caramel colour. (You have to stir all the time or the toffee will stick and burn.)

4. Remove the toffee from the heat and stir in the toasted nuts. Spread evenly over the chocolate base and transfer to the fridge to cool completely. This will take around an hour, although you can prepare this stage up to a day in advance.

5. For the topping, melt the chocolate in a heatproof bowl over a pan of simmering water, ensuring the bottom of the bowl doesn't touch the water. Stir in the vegetable oil to give it a shine and make it a little looser. Pour this over the caramel layer and smooth out, then transfer to the fridge to cool and set.

6. Cut into small squares. These will keep, covered, in the fridge for up to a week.

Rose and pistachio macaroons

◆•

These delicate pastel French fancies are world-famous, thanks to pâtisserie legends such as Pierre Hermé and Ladurée of Paris. My good friends Tim Kinnaird and Edd Kimber lead the Brit pack. Over the years I've picked up many tips for macaroons, and I've incorporated them into this recipe. Imagine these as a towering centrepiece, surrounded by pastel tea roses, or packed into a cellophane gift bag or basket. They are so versatile – that's the joy of macaroons. There are many possibilities for flavouring the filling, and you can change the colours of the shells to match the filling.

MAKES 24–30

- 150G/5½OZ/GENEROUS 1¼ CUPS ICING (CONFECTIONERS') SUGAR
- 150G/5½OZ/GENEROUS 1½ CUPS GROUND ALMONDS
- 275G/9¾OZ/GENEROUS 1¼ CUPS CASTER (SUPERFINE) SUGAR
- 115G/4OZ EGG WHITES, AGED IN THE FRIDGE FOR 48 HOURS (SEE TIP)
- A DROP OF GREEN OR PINK FOOD COLOURING

ROSE GANACHE

- 375G/13OZ WHITE CHOCOLATE, ROUGHLY CHOPPED
- 125ML/4FL OZ/½ CUP DOUBLE CREAM
- 6 TSP ROSE WATER, OR TO TASTE
- A DROP OF PINK FOOD COLOURING (OPTIONAL)
- 50G PISTACHIO NUTS, TOASTED AND FINELY CHOPPED

EGG WHITES
When making macaroons, it's a good idea to separate your eggs 48 hours in advance. Egg whites lose their elasticity with age, so they're easier to whip up without becoming grainy.

1. First, make the ganache. Melt the chocolate in a heatproof bowl over a pan of simmering water, ensuring the bottom of the bowl doesn't touch the water. Remove from the heat and stir in the cream and rose water, tasting to make sure the flavour is pronounced enough. Stir in the pink food colouring if you like. Chill for a few hours, until set.

2. Line a large baking sheet with baking parchment. Sift the icing sugar into a large bowl and add the almonds.

3. Put the caster sugar in a saucepan, add 5 tbsp water and bring to the boil. As soon as it boils, turn off the heat and leave for a minute.

4. Put the egg whites and green or pink food colouring in a separate clean, glass bowl and whisk until soft peaks form. Very slowly trickle the hot sugar mixture onto the egg whites, whisking continuously for a few minutes until glossy and thick. Fold in the icing sugar and almond mixture; the consistency should be loose.

5. Spoon the mixture into a piping bag with a plain nozzle, or snip the end off a disposable piping bag. Pipe small rounds, no bigger than 3.5cm/1¼in, spaced well apart, on the parchment. Leave to rest for 25 minutes to develop a skin – this will give the macaroons their distinctive shiny crust. Preheat the oven to 180°C/350°F/gas mark 4.

6. Bake the macaroons for 12 minutes. Slip the parchment off the baking sheet and leave to cool on a wire rack.

7. Spoon the chilled ganache into a piping bag with a plain tip and pipe into the centre of half the macaroon shells, sprinkle on the pistachios, sandwiching them together as you go. Store in an airtight container for up to a week.

Centrepiece pavlova

◆◆◆

This is my all-time favourite dessert – soft chewy meringue, beautifully sweet whipped cream and sharp, tangy fruits: it's got everything a dessert should have, without being too heavy. If things go wrong with your meringue, smash it up and turn the dish into Eton Mess. Before you begin, it's essential that all your equipment is spotlessly clean: any trace of grease will result in your egg whites not whipping up.

SERVES 6–8

- ◆ A LITTLE BUTTER, FOR GREASING
- ◆ 4 EGG WHITES
- ◆ 200G/7OZ/1 CUP CASTER (SUPERFINE) SUGAR
- ◆ 1 TSP CORNFLOUR (CORNSTARCH)
- ◆ 1 TSP WHITE-WINE VINEGAR

FILLING

- ◆ 150ML/5FL OZ/⅔ CUP DOUBLE CREAM
- ◆ 150G/5½OZ/GENEROUS ½ CUP MASCARPONE CHEESE
- ◆ 1 TSP VANILLA EXTRACT
- ◆ 25G/1OZ/2 TBSP CASTER (SUPERFINE) SUGAR
- ◆ 150G/5½OZ/GENEROUS 1 CUP RASPBERRIES
- ◆ 1 TBSP ICING (CONFECTIONERS') SUGAR
- ◆ SOFT FRUITS, SUCH AS RED BERRIES OR TROPICAL FRUITS

1. Preheat the oven to 170°C/325°F/gas mark 3. Lightly grease a baking sheet and line with greaseproof paper.

2. Whisk the egg whites in a clean, glass bowl until frothy, then gradually add the sugar, in three or four stages, whisking all the time until stiff peaks form. Whisk in the cornflour and vinegar. You should be able to hold the bowl upside-down without the meringue moving.

3. Spoon the meringue onto the prepared baking sheet, building it up nice and high, with a slightly flattened middle. Little and high is the way to go; don't make a huge circle – about 18cm/7in is perfect. Place in the oven, immediately turn the heat down to 140°C/275°F/gas mark 1 and bake for 1 hour, until crisp but not coloured.

4. Turn the oven off, open the door and leave the meringue in the oven to cool for around 30 minutes.

5. Carefully remove the meringue from the paper and place on your presentation plate.

6. To make the filling, whip the cream and mascarpone together until soft peaks form, then beat in the vanilla and sugar. Fill the middle of the meringue with the cream.

7. Put the raspberries and icing sugar in a pan over a low heat and cook gently until juices begin to flow; this won't take more than a minute. Crush a few raspberries to create more juice and spoon over the meringue, letting the juices run down the sides of the meringue.

8. Top with more fresh fruits and serve, or chill until you're ready to eat.

Nana Jean's fruit scones

I've been making these scones since I was knee-high. I'm not much taller now but I'm still true to this recipe I learned all those years ago. My nana used lard or margarine and bound the scones with water, as that's how her family showed her. When ingredients were rationed, people used whatever they could get. I prefer to use butter and cream as they make a better scone. Serve with your favourite jam and clotted cream for the ultimate British afternoon treat. You can swap the raisins for other fruit, such as dried apricots, and add a handful of toasted nuts if you like.

MAKES 10 SCONES

- 600G/1LB 5OZ/5 CUPS PLAIN (ALL-PURPOSE) FLOUR, PLUS EXTRA FOR DUSTING
- 4 TSP BAKING POWDER
- PINCH OF SALT
- 150G/5½OZ/GENEROUS ½ CUP UNSALTED BUTTER, COLD AND CUBED, PLUS EXTRA FOR GREASING
- 150G/5½OZ/¾ CUP CASTER (SUPERFINE) SUGAR
- 150G/5½OZ/SCANT 1 CUP CURRANTS OR RAISINS
- 2 EGGS
- 125ML/4FL OZ/½ CUP DOUBLE CREAM
- 125ML/4FL OZ/½ CUP WHOLE MILK, PLUS EXTRA TO GLAZE
- 1 TSP VANILLA EXTRACT (OPTIONAL)

1. Preheat the oven to 190°C/375°F/gas mark 5. Lightly grease a baking sheet.

2. Sift the flour, baking powder and salt into a large bowl or food processor. Add the butter and rub in or mix until it resembles breadcrumbs. Mix in the sugar and currants.

3. Beat the eggs, cream, milk and vanilla extract, if using, together. Pour them into the flour mixture and bring together lightly with your hands.

4. Turn the dough out onto a lightly floured surface and knead briefly to form a fairly smooth ball. It's important not to overwork the dough, as this will make tough scones; just bring it together with your hands and press lightly. Pat or gently roll the dough out to around 4cm/1½in thick. Dip a 5cm/2in diameter cutter in flour and use to stamp out rounds. Lightly gather together the remaining dough, reroll it and stamp out more scones.

5. Place the scones on the baking sheet, brush the tops with a little milk, and bake for about 20 minutes, or until risen and golden. Cool on a wire rack. Keep in an airtight container for up to 48 hours.

Turkish delight with pistachios

◆◆◆

As part of the vintage tea party I always present a cut-crystal bowl my Nana Jean gave me, filled with homemade Turkish delight and surrounded by dusty coral and pink tea roses and a pot of mint tea. Guests are so impressed with the beauty of the centrepiece, and I give little cellophane bags and pretty ribbons so they can pick their own pieces to take home after the party. This is a very simple recipe and should be made a day in advance as it needs time to set.

MAKES AROUND 30 PIECES

◆ VEGETABLE OIL, FOR GREASING
◆ 8 LEAVES OF GELATINE
◆ 450G/1LB/2¼ CUPS GRANULATED SUGAR
◆ 4–6 TBSP ROSE WATER
◆ 1–2 DROPS OF PINK FOOD COLOURING OR MORE IF YOU WANT A DARKER COLOUR
◆ 75G/2¾OZ/GENEROUS ½ CUP PISTACHIO NUTS, TOASTED
◆ 25G/1OZ/4 TBSP ICING (CONFECTIONERS') SUGAR
◆ 25G/1OZ/3 TBSP CORNFLOUR (CORNSTARCH)

1. You will need a 20cm/8in square container or tin. Don't use a loose-bottomed tin as the liquid will seep out. Lightly grease with oil, but don't line the tin.

2. Put the gelatine in a pan, add 300ml/10fl oz/1¼ cups water and leave for 5 minutes, until softened. When the gelatine is soft, place the pan over a medium heat and bring to a simmer, then cook, stirring, until the gelatine has melted. Add the sugar and stir until it has dissolved. Bring to the boil, then turn the heat down very low and simmer for 20 minutes. Keep an eye on it, as you might need to take it off the heat for a few seconds to stop the liquid bubbling over.

3. Take off the heat and stir in the rose water and food colouring. Taste the mixture: the rose flavour should be quite pronounced. The flavour will fade as the liquid cools, so you can afford to add a teaspoon more than you might think. Pour into the tin, then scatter in the pistachios. Chill overnight in the fridge.

4. The next day, sift together the icing sugar and cornflour and dust a work surface with a little of the mixture. Carefully slide a knife around the sides of the Turkish delight and turn out onto the work surface. Peel back the cling film and discard. Cut the Turkish delight into pieces, using a shaped cutter if you like, then toss with the rest of the icing sugar mixture to coat liberally. Serve.

Cheese and leek scones

◆•◆

This is a beautiful light scone recipe; the cayenne adds a little kick that complements the cheese and leek. These always feature at my vintage tea parties. It's nice to have a selection of savoury things as well as sweet, and these go down a treat served warm with a pot of butter.

MAKES 10 SCONES

- 1 TBSP VEGETABLE OIL, PLUS EXTRA FOR GREASING
- 140G/5OZ/GENEROUS ½ CUP UNSALTED BUTTER, COLD AND CUBED, PLUS 15G/½OZ/1 TBSP AND EXTRA FOR GREASING
- 1 LEEK, CLEANED AND FINELY SLICED
- 550G/1LB 4OZ/4½ CUPS SELF-RAISING FLOUR, PLUS EXTRA FOR DUSTING
- 1 TSP CAYENNE PEPPER
- GOOD PINCH OF SALT
- 150G/5½OZ/1¼ CUPS MATURE CHEDDAR CHEESE, GRATED, PLUS EXTRA FOR SPRINKLING
- 125G/4½OZ/½ CUP PLAIN YOGURT
- 200ML/7FL OZ/GENEROUS ¾ CUP MILK

1. Preheat the oven to 200°C/400°F/gas mark 6. Lightly grease a baking sheet with oil.

2. Heat the oil in a pan, add the 15g/½oz/1 tbsp butter and the leek. Cover and cook over a medium-low heat for about 10 minutes, until the leek is soft but not coloured. Set aside to cool slightly.

3. Sift together the flour, cayenne and salt. Using your fingertips, lightly rub in the 140g/5oz/generous ½ cup butter until the mixture resembles breadcrumbs. (Alternatively, put the ingredients in a food processor and pulse.)

4. Stir in the leeks and cheese and then the yogurt and most of the milk to make a soft dough – keep back a little milk for brushing the tops of the scones. It's important not to overwork the dough, as this will make tough scones; just bring the mixture together with your hands and press lightly.

5. Turn onto a lightly floured work surface and pat out to around 4cm/1½in thick. Dip a 5cm/2in diameter cutter in flour and use it to stamp out rounds. Gather together the remaining dough, reroll it and stamp out more scones to use it all up.

6. Place the scones on the baking sheet, brush the tops with the reserved milk and sprinkle on some more cheese. Bake for 15–20 minutes, until well-risen and golden. Cool on a wire rack. Eat warm or cold with good butter. Store in an airtight container for up to 48 hours.

Homity pie

This is a traditional British pie, created during World War II to make the most of available ingredients during rationing. There was always a homity pie on our Saturday afternoon tea table. It's essentially a cheese and potato pie. My family recipe includes sweet softened onions, but leeks can be used, too. Use the best mature Cheddar you can get.

SERVES 8–10

- 1 X 20CM/8IN BLIND-BAKED SHORTCRUST PASTRY CASE (PAGE 17 BUT OMIT THE SUGAR)
- 1KG/2LB 4OZ FLOURY (STARCHY) POTATOES, PEELED AND CHOPPED
- 100ML/3½FL OZ/6–7 TBSP DOUBLE CREAM
- 25G/1OZ/2 TBSP UNSALTED BUTTER
- 1 TBSP VEGETABLE OIL
- 1 LARGE WHITE ONION, THINLY SLICED
- ½ CLOVE GARLIC, FINELY CHOPPED
- 600G/1LB 5OZ GOOD MATURE CHEDDAR CHEESE, GRATED
- SALT AND FRESHLY GROUND BLACK PEPPER

1. Make and bake the pastry case on page 17, using a deep 20cm/8in round loose-bottomed or springform cake tin, and blind-bake according to the recipe. (Although the tin is deeper, the same rules apply. Don't worry about the pastry round the edges of the tin – if it looks rugged it adds to the rustic look of the pie.)

2. Boil the potatoes until tender. Drain thoroughly, add the cream and then mash.

3. Melt the butter and oil in a frying pan over a low heat, and when hot, add the onion and garlic. Cover with a lid and cook for around 10 minutes. This slow cooking slightly caramelizes the onion and makes it beautifully sweet. Stir from time to time.

4. Put the mashed potatoes, onion and three-quarters of the cheese in a large bowl and season well to taste. Fill the baked pastry shell with the potato mixture, sprinkle with the remaining cheese and bake at 190°C/375°F/gas mark 5 for 45 minutes.

5. Push up the loose bottom and slide the pie off the base, or open the clip on the springform tin. Leave to cool slightly on a wire rack and serve warm. This will keep in the fridge for around 5 days. Perfect with coleslaw and a salad for a spring weekend lunch.

Homemade pork pies with cheat's piccalilli

As the spring approaches, I think of picnics and lazy afternoons in the park or on my local beach. Picnic pork pies are a doddle to make. They're perfect for afternoon tea with my simple piccalilli. This piccalilli can be made in advance and it keeps in the fridge for up to 2 months, to enjoy with cold cuts and on sandwiches.

MAKES 6 PIES

- 600G/1LB 5OZ BONED SHOULDER OF PORK, WITH A GOOD MARBLING OF FAT, FINELY CHOPPED
- SALT AND FRESHLY GROUND BLACK PEPPER
- 1 TSP CHOPPED FRESH SAGE

HOT-WATER CRUST PASTRY

- 500G/1LB 2OZ/4 CUPS PLAIN (ALL-PURPOSE) FLOUR, PLUS EXTRA FOR DUSTING
- 175G/6OZ/¾ CUP LARD, ROUGHLY CUBED
- 1 EGG, BEATEN, TO GLAZE

PICCALILLI

- 200ML/7FL OZ/GENEROUS ¾ CUP WHITE-WINE VINEGAR
- 60G/2¼OZ/5 TBSP CASTER (SUPERFINE) SUGAR
- 1 TSP HORSERADISH SAUCE
- 1 LARGE RED CHILLI, DESEEDED AND FINELY CHOPPED
- 2 PEPPERS, ANY COLOUR, FINELY CUBED
- ¼ CUCUMBER, PEELED, DESEEDED AND FINELY CUBED
- 1 COURGETTE, FINELY CUBED
- 2 CELERY STALKS, FINELY CUBED
- 50G/1¾OZ PICKLED ONIONS (THE SMALLEST YOU CAN FIND)
- 1 TBSP CORNFLOUR (CORNSTARCH)
- 1 TBSP GROUND TURMERIC
- 3 TBSP DIJON MUSTARD

1. For the piccalilli, combine the vinegar, sugar, horseradish and half the chilli in a pan. Heat gently until the sugar has dissolved, then bring to the boil. Simmer for 2 minutes. Set aside to cool, then strain and reserve the vinegar.

2. Put all the vegetables in a large bowl and add the pickled onions.

3. Put the remaining chilli in a small bowl, add 3 tsp salt, the cornflour, turmeric and mustard and mix with about 3 tbsp of the flavoured vinegar. Bring the rest of the vinegar to the boil, then stir in the chilli mixture. Cook for 2–3 minutes, stirring, until thickened. Pour the hot mixture over the vegetables and mix thoroughly. Leave to cool and then transfer to sterilized jars or resealable plastic containers and store in the fridge.

4. For the pies, preheat the oven to 200°C/400°F/gas mark 6. To prepare the filling, season the pork with about 1 tbsp salt, 1 tsp pepper and the sage.

5. To make the pastry: mix the flour and 1 tsp salt in a bowl and make a well in the centre. Put the lard in a pan with 200ml/7fl oz/generous ¾ cup water and bring to the boil, then stir it into the flour with a wooden spoon to form a smooth dough. Cover and leave for about 15 minutes, or until cool enough to handle.

6. Divide the dough into 6 equal pieces. Divide each piece into 2 balls, one for the base of the pie and a slightly smaller one for the lid. On a lightly floured work surface, roll out the larger piece to a circle 12–14cm/5in in diameter. Roll out the smaller piece to a circle about 6cm/2½in in diameter.

7. Put one-sixth of the filling in the centre of the larger circle, lay the smaller circle on top and raise the sides of the larger one up, then pinch the lid and sides together with your fingers. Repeat with the rest of the pastry and filling.

8. Brush the pies all over with beaten egg, make a small hole in the middle and cook for 35 minutes, until golden. Check after 25 minutes, and if they are getting too brown, cover them with foil. Leave to cool completely on a wire rack. Serve with the piccalilli – and lashings of it.

Spring & Easter

◆◆◆◆◆◆◆◆◆◆◆◆◆◆◆◆◆◆◆◆◆◆◆

Spring and baking go together like Sonny and Cher. It's perhaps the greatest baking season of them all, with so many occasions: Mother's Day, Easter, fêtes and festivals. Plus for me it's the time when my scooter, Shimmy, comes out of hibernation after the winter. I always think of the spring as the time I'm 'allowed' to bake indulgently again, after several failed months of New Year resolution dieting...

◆◆◆◆◆◆◆◆◆◆◆◆◆◆◆◆◆◆◆◆◆◆◆

Glazed lemon tart

There is no better way to finish a spring evening meal than with a slice of lemon tart, the creamy lemon custard sharp and bursting with flavour. This is one of those dishes that screams summer is on its way. It's essential to blind-bake your pastry case before you add the filling so that the pastry is crisp. Glazing the tart adds another texture, with a thin, crisp topping; you don't have to do it if you don't feel confident, or don't have a blowtorch, but it does look really beautiful. I serve this with new-season strawberries at the end of May, or with raspberries, passion fruit and a scoop of vanilla ice cream for one of my all-time favourite desserts.

MAKES 1 X 21CM/8IN TART

- 5 EGGS
- 125G/4½OZ/GENEROUS ½ CUP CASTER (SUPERFINE) SUGAR
- GRATED ZEST AND JUICE OF 3 UNWAXED LEMONS
- 250ML/9FL OZ/GENEROUS 1 CUP DOUBLE CREAM
- 1 X 21CM/8IN BLIND-BAKED SWEET PASTRY CASE (PAGE 17, BUT I MAKE IT 2.5CM/1IN DEEP)
- 3 TBSP DEMERARA SUGAR, TO GLAZE

1. Preheat the oven to 150°C/300°F/gas mark 2. Lightly whisk the eggs and sugar together. Trickle in the lemon juice, whisking continuously to prevent the mixture from curdling. Gently stir in the cream and lemon zest – you don't want a lot of bubbles in your mixture as you need the finished tart to be smooth. Leave to settle for 5 minutes, to get rid of any remaining bubbles.

2. Put the pastry case in its tin on a baking sheet. Fill it with the lemon custard, carefully transfer to the oven and bake for 30–40 minutes. The tart should be set but still have a slight wobble in the middle. Chill for at least 2 hours.

3. To glaze, liberally dust the tart with demerara sugar, then blast with a blowtorch until bubbling and caramelized. Alternatively, caramelize under a blistering-hot grill, but keep an eye on it as grill heat can be patchy. Leave to cool before serving.

Lemon drizzle poppy seed loaf

◆◆◆

This afternoon cake is sweet, sour, sticky and moist – and you won't believe how simple the drizzle glaze is. You can leave out the poppy seeds if you like. Every time I see my Nana Jean she always says 'Have you made a lemon drizzle for me pet?'

MAKES 1 X 900G/2LB LOAF OR 1 X 20CM/8IN ROUND CAKE

◆ 200G/7OZ/GENEROUS ¾ CUP UNSALTED BUTTER, AT ROOM TEMPERATURE, PLUS EXTRA FOR GREASING
◆ 200G/7OZ/1 CUP CASTER (SUPERFINE) SUGAR
◆ 3 EGGS
◆ 175G/6OZ/1½ CUPS SELF-RAISING FLOUR, PLUS EXTRA FOR DUSTING
◆ 15G/½OZ/2 TBSP CORNFLOUR (CORNSTARCH)
◆ GRATED ZEST OF 2 UNWAXED LEMONS
◆ 1 TSP POPPY SEEDS (OPTIONAL)
◆ 1 TBSP LEMON CURD

LEMON DRIZZLE

◆ JUICE OF 2 LEMONS
◆ 1 TBSP LEMON CURD
◆ 50G/1¾OZ/¼ CUP CASTER (SUPERFINE) SUGAR

1. Preheat the oven to 180°C/350°F/gas mark 4. Grease a 900g/2lb loaf tin or 20cm/8in diameter cake tin, dust it with flour, then turn it upside-down and tap to remove any excess flour.

2. Beat the butter for a minute or so, until light and fluffy. Add the sugar and beat until incorporated. Scrape down the bowl to ensure all the ingredients are combined. Beat in the eggs one at a time, adding 1 tbsp flour after each egg to keep the mixture smooth.

3. Sift the remaining flour and the cornflour together, then mix in the lemon zest and poppy seeds, if using. Slowly add these dry ingredients to the butter-and-egg mixture. Scrape down the bowl to ensure everything is evenly mixed, then add the lemon curd and quickly beat to combine – do not overbeat. Spoon the mixture into the tin and level the top.

4. Bake the loaf for 45 minutes, until a knife or skewer comes out clean. (A round cake will take less time as it's thinner, so check it after 30 minutes.)

5. To make the lemon drizzle, put the lemon juice, lemon curd and sugar in a pan over a low heat until the sugar has dissolved. Bring to the boil, then boil for 10–20 seconds, until syrupy, and leave for 2 minutes to thicken. Brush onto or pour over the warm cake. For added zing, stab the cake all over with a skewer before pouring on the syrup.

Popcorn lemon cracker whoopee pies

◆-◆

Whoopee pies are a traditional Amish dessert, allegedly named because the Amish men, on finding the cake in their bait boxes, would declare 'Whoopee!' I've taken a few of my favourite flavours – popcorn, lemon and toffee – and combined them deliciously in this dessert. These will make a wonderful addition to any Easter picnic.

MAKES 6 PIES

WHOOPEE PIES

◆ 175G/6OZ/¾ CUP UNSALTED BUTTER, AT ROOM TEMPERATURE, PLUS EXTRA FOR GREASING

◆ 150G/5½OZ/¾ CUP DARK BROWN SUGAR

◆ 1 EGG

◆ 115G/4OZ/GENEROUS ¼ CUP GOLDEN SYRUP (LIGHT CORN SYRUP)

◆ 1 TSP VANILLA EXTRACT

◆ 375G/13OZ/3 CUPS PLAIN (ALL-PURPOSE) FLOUR

◆ 1 TSP BICARBONATE OF SODA (BAKING SODA)

TOFFEE

◆ 40G/1½OZ/3 TBSP UNSALTED BUTTER

◆ 40G/1½OZ/3 TBSP SOFT DARK BROWN SUGAR

◆ 3 TBSP DOUBLE CREAM

FILLING AND TOPPING

◆ 50G PACK OF TOFFEE POPCORN, SMASHED UP

◆ 70G/2½OZ/5 TBSP UNSALTED BUTTER, AT ROOM TEMPERATURE

◆ 85G/3OZ/6 TBSP FULL-FAT SOFT CHEESE

◆ 225G/8OZ/2 CUPS ICING (CONFECTIONERS') SUGAR

◆ GRATED ZEST OF 1 UNWAXED LEMON

◆ POPPING CANDY (OPTIONAL)

◆ EDIBLE GLITTER OR COLOURED SPRINKLES (OPTIONAL)

1. Preheat the oven to 180°C/350°F/gas mark 4. Grease a baking sheet. Beat the butter for a minute or so, until light and fluffy. Add the brown sugar and beat until incorporated. Scrape down the bowl to ensure all the ingredients are combined. Beat in the egg, followed by the golden syrup and vanilla.

2. Sift the flour with the bicarbonate of soda, then slowly beat it into the butter-and-sugar mixture. Scrape down the bowl to ensure everything is evenly mixed; the dough will be dry and stiff.

3. Take a small handful of the dough and roll into a 5cm/2in ball. Repeat until you have 12 balls. Set the balls on the baking sheet and flatten slightly with your hands. Bake for 13–15 minutes, until risen, golden and firm to the touch. Leave to cool.

4. To make the toffee, put the butter and sugar in a pan, bring to the boil, then add the cream and boil for another minute. Dip 6 of the whoopees in the toffee, scatter with the smashed-up popcorn and leave to cool.

5. To make the filling, beat the butter and soft cheese together until combined (don't overbeat) and then add the icing sugar and lemon zest and beat until creamy. Add a good dollop of the filling to the remaining 6 whoopees. Sprinkle on the popping candy, if using.

6. Place the toffee-and-popcorn-coated tops on the filled bottoms and press lightly. Sprinkle with edible glitter or coloured sprinkles, if using, for added kitsch.

Mocha Napoleons

◆◆

Chocolate and coffee are best friends – they really complement each other – so I wanted a recipe that included both. Napoleons are French layered pastries filled with a ganache. Think of it as a funky custard slice. You can enjoy these in the spring in all flavours: lemon, custard and, of course, mocha.

SERVES 4

◆ 100G/3½OZ/7 TBSP UNSALTED BUTTER
◆ 50G/1¾OZ COCOA POWDER
◆ 275G PACK OF FILO PASTRY
◆ 100G/3½OZ/½ CUP CASTER (SUPERFINE) SUGAR

GANACHE

◆ 250ML/9FL OZ/GENEROUS 1 CUP WHOLE MILK
◆ 3 TSP GROUND COFFEE
◆ 200G/7OZ DARK CHOCOLATE (70% COCOA SOLIDS), FINELY CHOPPED

TO SERVE

◆ LIGHTLY WHIPPED CREAM, SWEETENED WITH A LITTLE CASTER (SUPERFINE) SUGAR
◆ ICING (CONFECTIONERS') SUGAR, FOR DUSTING
◆ TOASTED HAZELNUTS, VERY FINELY CHOPPED

1. Preheat the oven to 180°C/350°F/gas mark 4. Line a baking sheet with baking parchment. Melt the butter in a small pan, add the cocoa and stir.

2. Lay a sheet of filo pastry on your work surface and brush with the cocoa butter. Lay a second sheet of filo on top and brush with more cocoa butter. Lay these 2 sheets on the baking sheet and sprinkle over half the sugar. Using a sharp knife, cut the filo into 8 rectangles so that you know where to break it once cooked. Cover with baking parchment.

3. Repeat the process with 2 more sheets of filo pastry and the remaining sugar, laying them on top of the baking parchment. Cover with more baking parchment, then put another baking sheet on top. So you will have the following layers: baking sheet, parchment, 2 sheets of dough, parchment, 2 sheets of dough, parchment, baking sheet. Bake for 15 minutes, until golden and crisp.

4. Meanwhile, make the ganache. Warm the milk in a saucepan, stir in the coffee and simmer over a very low heat for 5 minutes. Put the chocolate in a heatproof bowl. Strain the milk, discarding the coffee grounds. Immediately pour the warm, coffee-scented milk over the chocolate and stir until melted. Cover the bowl with cling film and place in the fridge to set.

5. Leave the pastry to cool. Snap or cut the cooked pastry into the marked rectangles so you end up with 16 pieces of chocolate pastry.

6. Dab a little of the ganache onto 4 serving plates. Place a piece of pastry on the ganache, which will stop it slipping. Cover with ganache and whipped cream, either piped or spread with a spoon, then pastry, more ganache and whipped cream and finally pastry. Dust with icing sugar and scatter the nuts over the napoleons. You'll have a few spare pieces of pastry, a chef's treat to eat later with peanut butter. (Or is that just me?)

Super-fast white chocolate cheesecake with hokey-pokey

◆◆

This is a dinner-party dish you can whip up in 5 minutes. Make sure your cream cheese is out of the fridge in advance or it will go lumpy when you beat it. If this happens, you'll have a more textured filling rather than a very smooth one. The hokey-pokey (it's basically honeycomb toffee, like a Crunchie bar) looks great, adds texture, and is magic to make, too! I learnt when I was a kid and I'll never forget seeing the golden clouds billowing out of the pan. Proper fantastic stuff.

MAKES 1 X 20CM/8IN ROUND CHEESECAKE

GINGER BASE

◆ 200G/7OZ GINGERSNAP BISCUITS, SMASHED TO FINE CRUMBS
◆ 70G/2½OZ/5 TBSP UNSALTED BUTTER, MELTED

FILLING

◆ 250G/9OZ/GENEROUS 1 CUP FULL-FAT SOFT CHEESE, AT ROOM TEMPERATURE
◆ 250G/9OZ/GENEROUS 1 CUP MASCARPONE
◆ 100G/3½OZ/½ CUP CASTER (SUPERFINE) SUGAR
◆ 100ML/3½FL OZ DOUBLE CREAM
◆ 500G/1LB 2OZ WHITE CHOCOLATE, BROKEN INTO PIECES

HOKEY POKEY (OPTIONAL)

◆ VEGETABLE OIL, FOR GREASING
◆ 75G/2¾OZ/⅓ CUP CASTER (SUPERFINE) SUGAR
◆ 3 TBSP GOLDEN SYRUP (LIGHT CORN SYRUP)
◆ 1 TSP BICARBONATE OF SODA (BAKING SODA)

1. First, make the base. Line a 20cm/8in round loose-bottomed tart tin. Stir the biscuit crumbs into the melted butter and press evenly into the tin. Put the base in the fridge.

2. Put all the filling ingredients into the bowl of a food mixer and beat together for 2 minutes, or until smooth and thickened. The mixture needs to be spreadable but not too loose. Spoon the filling over the base and smooth out. Cover the cheesecake and put it in the fridge to set for at least an hour.

3. To make the hokey-pokey, lightly oil a large piece of baking parchment. Put the sugar and syrup into a saucepan and stir. Put the pan over a low heat until the sugar dissolves, then turn up the heat and bring to the boil. After about 3 minutes it will turn into a bubbling mass of amber.

4. Take the pan off the heat and whisk in the bicarbonate of soda. The mix will instantly form billowing clouds of gold. Immediately turn it out onto the baking parchment and leave to set. Once set, bash it up into shards and scatter the hokey-pokey over the cheesecake. This cheesecake will keep in an airtight tin for up to 4 days.

THE TART TIN
Shallow tins are best for cheesecakes as they allow you to get a really flat surface. Using a large palette knife, you can smooth the cheesecake level with the sides of the tin.

Chocolate and pistachio biscotti

◆◆

These wonderful crisp, light Italian biscotti are deep in flavour and spiked with chocolate chips and nuts.

MAKES 15-20 BISCUITS

- 90G/3¼OZ/6 TBSP UNSALTED BUTTER, AT ROOM TEMPERATURE, PLUS EXTRA FOR GREASING
- 225G/8OZ/GENEROUS 1 CUP CASTER (SUPERFINE) SUGAR
- 2 EGGS
- 250G/9OZ/2 CUPS PLAIN (ALL-PURPOSE) FLOUR
- 1 TSP BICARBONATE OF SODA (BAKING SODA)
- 60G/2¼OZ COCOA POWDER
- PINCH OF SALT
- 150G/5½OZ PISTACHIO NUTS, TOASTED
- 100G/3½OZ MILK CHOCOLATE CHIPS

1. Preheat the oven to 180°C/350°F/gas mark 4. Grease a baking sheet.

2. Beat the butter for a minute or so, until light and fluffy. Add the sugar and beat until incorporated. Scrape down the bowl to ensure all the ingredients are combined. Beat in the eggs one at a time, adding 1 tbsp flour after each egg to keep the mixture smooth.

3. Sift together the remaining flour, bicarbonate of soda, cocoa and salt, then mix in the pistachios and chocolate chips. Slowly mix into the butter-and-egg mixture to make a stiff dough. Scrape down the bowl to ensure everything is evenly mixed, then give the dough one final beat (don't overbeat it).

4. Transfer the dough to the baking sheet and form it into a log shape about 28 x 10cm/11 x 4in. Flatten slightly with your hands and bake for 25 minutes, until just firm but not solid. Leave to cool on the baking sheet for 10 minutes.

5. Turn the oven down to 150°C/300°F/gas mark 2. Transfer the dough to a cutting board. Using a sharp bread knife, carefully cut your biscotti at an angle in 1.5cm/½in thick slices. Don't worry if they break up; just squidge them back together and they'll reattach when baked for the second time. Place the biscotti back on the baking sheet and cook for an additional 8–10 minutes, until crisp. Leave to cool completely on a wire rack before dunking in coffee and eating.

ALSO TRY...
There are many biscotti variations: almonds and cranberries, hazelnut and chocolate, orange and pecan... use the same weight as specified above.

Syrup-soaked coffee and walnut cake

During spring and Easter I often get asked for charity donations for coffee mornings and fêtes. I always bake one of these to sell by the slice. This is a recipe my Aunty Josephine gave me, but I've put a modern spin on it with the coffee syrup. You can use instant coffee made with boiling water or a good espresso – the better the coffee, the better the flavour of the cake.

MAKES 1 X 20CM/8IN ROUND CAKE
- 325G/11½OZ/1½ CUPS UNSALTED BUTTER, AT ROOM TEMPERATURE, PLUS EXTRA FOR GREASING
- 300G/10½OZ/1½ CUPS SOFT LIGHT BROWN SUGAR
- 6 EGGS
- 300G/10½OZ/SCANT 2½ CUPS SELF-RAISING FLOUR, SIFTED
- 35G/1¼OZ/¼ CUP CORNFLOUR (CORNSTARCH)
- 100G/3½OZ/1 CUP WALNUT PIECES, TOASTED AND ROUGHLY CHOPPED, PLUS WALNUT HALVES, TO DECORATE
- 1 TSP VANILLA EXTRACT
- 3 TSP INSTANT COFFEE DISSOLVED IN 3 TBSP BOILING WATER

COFFEE SYRUP
- 3 TBSP STRONG BLACK COFFEE
- 3 TBSP TIA MARIA
- 25G/1OZ/2 TBSP CASTER (SUPERFINE) SUGAR

COFFEE BUTTERCREAM
- 225G/8OZ/1 CUP UNSALTED BUTTER, AT ROOM TEMPERATURE
- 125ML/4½FL OZ/GENEROUS ½ CUP STRONG BLACK COFFEE
- 1 TSP VANILLA EXTRACT
- 1KG/2LB 4OZ/8½ CUPS ICING (CONFECTIONERS') SUGAR

1. Preheat the oven to 180°C/350°F/gas mark 4. Grease 2 x 20cm/8in diameter cake tins and line with baking parchment.

2. Beat the butter for a minute or so, until light and fluffy. Add the sugar and beat until incorporated. Scrape down the bowl to ensure all the ingredients are combined. Beat in the eggs one at a time, adding 1 tbsp flour after each egg to keep the mixture smooth.

3. Sift the remaining flour and the cornflour together and toss the walnut pieces in the flour (this will prevent them from sinking in the cake). Slowly mix this and the vanilla into the butter-and-egg mixture. Fold in the coffee. Scrape down the bowl to ensure everything is evenly mixed, then divide the mixture between the 2 tins. Bake for 35–45 minutes. Test after about 35 minutes: when it's cooked, a knife or skewer inserted into the centre will come out clean. Leave to cool in the tins for 10 minutes, then turn out onto a wire rack.

4. To make the syrup, put the coffee, Tia Maria and sugar in a pan over a medium-low heat and cook, stirring, until the sugar is dissolved.

5. While the cakes are still warm, drizzle the syrup over the sponge so it soaks in. You may not need all the syrup, and it's nice to keep some back for the top of the cake.

6. To make the coffee buttercream, beat the butter until softened, then add the coffee, vanilla and icing sugar and beat for several minutes, until creamy and thick.

7. Sandwich the cake with half the buttercream and use the remaining buttercream to cover the top. Decorate with walnut halves and a drizzle of the syrup if you wish.

Double-chocolate s'mores cookies

These originated as an American campfire treat back in the 1920s – toasted marshmallows and chocolate sandwiched between 2 graham crackers (similar to British digestives). They are pretty awesome and I've never seen anything like them in the UK, so I hope you love them as much as I do.

MAKES 24 SMALL COOKIES

- 225G/8OZ/1 CUP UNSALTED BUTTER, AT ROOM TEMPERATURE, PLUS EXTRA FOR GREASING
- 325G/11½OZ/GENEROUS 1½ CUPS CASTER (SUPERFINE) SUGAR
- 2 EGGS
- 250G/9OZ/2 CUPS PLAIN (ALL-PURPOSE) FLOUR
- 2 TSP BAKING POWDER
- 1 TSP BICARBONATE OF SODA (BAKING SODA)
- 70G/2½OZ COCOA POWDER
- 150G/5½OZ CHOCOLATE CHIPS
- 200G/7OZ MILK CHOCOLATE, BROKEN INTO PIECES
- 12 LARGE MARSHMALLOWS, HALVED

1. Preheat the oven to 180°C/350°F/gas mark 4. Grease 2 baking sheets.

2. Beat the butter for a minute or so, until light and fluffy. Add the sugar and beat until incorporated. Scrape down the bowl to ensure all the ingredients are combined. Beat in the eggs one at a time, adding 1 tbsp flour after each egg to keep the mixture smooth.

3. Sift together the remaining flour, the baking powder, bicarbonate of soda and cocoa, then stir in the chocolate chips. Slowly beat the dry ingredients into the butter and egg mixture. Scrape down the bowl to ensure everything is evenly mixed, then give a final stir. The mixture will be quite dry.

4. Take heaped teaspoons of the mixture and roll into 24 balls. Place the balls on the prepared baking sheet, spaced a few inches apart as they will spread. Pat the balls to flatten slightly and bake for 8 minutes. Put the chocolate in a large heatproof bowl and melt over a pan of simmering water, making sure the bowl doesn't touch the water.

5. Drizzle the cookies with the melted chocolate and place a marshmallow, cut side down, on top of each cookie. Place under a hot grill for a minute or so, until the marshmallows begin to turn golden. Transfer to a wire rack to cool. They will keep in an airtight container for up to 7 days.

Elvis Bars

I've always respected Elvis, for two reasons: first, because he pulled Priscilla, one of the most beautiful, iconic women in the world, and secondly because he loved food. I first saw these bars made by American baker Ina Garten. I've changed a few things and added more peanut butter. Would the King approve? Of course.

MAKES 12 BARS

- 225G/8OZ/1 CUP UNSALTED BUTTER, AT ROOM TEMPERATURE, PLUS EXTRA FOR GREASING
- 225G/8OZ/GENEROUS 1 CUP CASTER (SUPERFINE) SUGAR
- 2 EGGS
- 450G/1LB/1¾ CUPS SMOOTH PEANUT BUTTER
- 350G/12OZ/SCANT 3 CUPS PLAIN (ALL-PURPOSE) FLOUR
- 1 TSP BAKING POWDER
- PINCH OF SALT
- 5 TBSP RASPBERRY JAM
- FEW HANDFULS OF SALTED PEANUTS, COARSELY CHOPPED

1. Preheat the oven to 180°C/350°F/gas mark 4. Grease a 33 x 20cm/13 x 8in baking tin and line with baking parchment.

2. Using a food mixer with the paddle attachment, cream the butter and sugar together at a medium speed for about 2 minutes, until light and fluffy.

3. Scrape down the bowl. With the mixer at a low speed, add the eggs and peanut butter and mix until combined.

4. In a bowl, sift together the flour, baking powder and salt. With the mixer at a low speed, gradually add the flour mixture to the peanut butter mixture and mix until combined.

5. Spoon two-thirds of the mixture into the prepared tin and spread evenly, using clean hands. Spread the jam over the dough, leaving a 2.5cm/1in margin so the jam doesn't burn around the edges. Drop small balls of the remaining peanut butter mixture evenly over the jam. Don't worry if all the jam isn't covered, as the mixture will spread in the oven. Sprinkle with chopped peanuts and bake for 30 minutes, until golden brown. The bars will still be soft, but they will harden slightly as they cool. Leave to cool in the tin.

6. Cut into squares. They will keep in an airtight container for up to 7 days.

Ernie's whisky tea loaf

My beloved Granda Ernie was a big whisky drinker and cake eater, so this recipe is for him. This cake includes dried fruits soaked in copious amounts of tea and whisky, so it is full of plump fruits bursting with a beautiful flavour. Strangely there's no butter in it. I imagine that's because it wasn't readily available, but it works perfectly without it, so I'm not going to start chopping and changing. The method is also incredibly simple. My Nana Jean had no one to impress with her writing, so she just kept it basic and to the point.

MAKES 1 X 900G/2LB LOAF

- 400G/14OZ/2½ CUPS DRIED FRUITS – SULTANAS (GOLDEN RAISINS), CURRANTS, MIXED (CANDIED) PEEL
- 150ML/5FL OZ/⅔ CUP WHISKY
- 150ML/5FL OZ/⅔ CUP STRONG BREWED TEA, TEPID
- VEGETABLE OIL, FOR GREASING
- 200G/7OZ/1 CUP SOFT DARK BROWN SUGAR
- 225G/8OZ/1¾ CUPS SELF-RAISING FLOUR, SIFTED, PLUS EXTRA FOR DUSTING
- 1 EGG, BEATEN
- 1 TSP MIXED SPICE (APPLE PIE SPICE)

1. Put the dried fruits in a large bowl and pour over the whisky and tea. Leave overnight or for at least 6 hours, so the fruits soak up the flavours and become plump.

2. Preheat the oven to 170°C/325°F/gas mark 3. Grease and flour a 900g/2lb loaf tin.

3. Add the sugar, flour, egg and spice to the soaked fruit, stir well with a wooden spoon, then spoon into the loaf tin and bake for 1½ hours. (After about 50 minutes, check the cake and if the top is browning too quickly, cover the top with foil.) Test it is cooked by inserting a skewer; if it comes out clean the cake is done. Leave to cool on a wire rack.

4. The loaf will keep in an airtight container for a week or so. Serve sliced and slathered in butter with a cup of strong tea.

Granda Ernie

Brioche with glazed apricots

◆◆◆

I adore brioche. I always thought it would be difficult to make, but it's quite straight-forward, especially if you use a food mixer with a dough hook. Adding fruit makes the soft, sweet bread even more moist as the juices run into the dough. The apricots lighten the loaf beautifully. This is a great breakfast dish for a lazy weekend treat. I also love it on a sunny day while sitting in the garden with a glass of Pimm's.

MAKES 1 X 900G/2LB LOAF

◆ 400G/14OZ/3¼ CUPS STRONG WHITE BREAD FLOUR, PLUS EXTRA FOR DUSTING
◆ GRATED ZEST OF 1 UNWAXED LEMON
◆ 1 TSP SEA SALT
◆ 6 TBSP WHOLE MILK
◆ 17G SACHET DRIED YEAST OR 14G FRESH YEAST
◆ 50G/1¾OZ/¼ CUP CASTER (SUPERFINE) SUGAR
◆ 115G/4OZ/½ CUP UNSALTED BUTTER, AT ROOM TEMPERATURE, CUBED, PLUS EXTRA FOR GREASING
◆ 4 EGGS, BEATEN

APRICOT TOPPING

◆ 3 APRICOTS
◆ 150G/5½OZ/¾ CUP CASTER (SUPERFINE) SUGAR
◆ 1 TBSP APRICOT JAM OR MARMALADE
◆ SEEDS SCRAPED FROM 1 VANILLA POD
◆ 2 TSP DEMERARA SUGAR

LEFTOVERS
Never throw a brioche away. Use any stale leftovers to make a bread pudding or bread-and-butter pudding.

1. Put the flour, lemon zest and salt in a bowl and toss well.

2. Warm the milk in a pan until tepid, then remove from the heat. Add the yeast and sugar, stir and leave for 5 minutes to activate the yeast.

3. Pour the warm liquid into the bowl containing the dry ingredients and slowly mix it into the flour. Add the butter and mix until it is incorporated. Mix in the eggs one at a time; the dough should be a little wet.

4. Turn the dough out onto a floured surface and knead for 10 minutes. Lightly butter the mixing bowl and put the dough back in. Cover with cling film and chill for 1 hour.

5. Lightly butter your loaf tin. Shape the chilled dough into a loaf and place in the tin. Cover with cling film and leave in a warm, draught-free place to rise for 1 hour.

6. While the dough is rising, make the topping. Put the apricots in a bowl of boiling water for a few minutes, then cut them in half, slip their skins off and remove the stones. Put the caster sugar, jam, vanilla seeds and 150ml/5fl oz water in a saucepan and boil for 2 minutes to make a syrup. Add the apricots and poach for a few minutes; they will be cooked further in the oven, so you don't want them to become too soft. Leave to cool; the syrup will thicken nicely as it cools.

7. Preheat the oven to 200°C/400°F/gas mark 6. When the dough has almost doubled in size, place the apricots on top of the brioche, cut-side-down. Reserve the poaching syrup. Sprinkle the demerara sugar over the apricots.

8. Bake the brioche for 10 minutes, then turn the oven down to 180°C/350°F/gas mark 4 and bake for a further 25 minutes, or until golden brown. Turn out of the tin and leave to cool on a wire rack. To serve, spoon over the reserved apricot syrup.

Spinach, ricotta and pine nut parcels

These are great for a picnic. I love picky food: small bites are lovely instead of a large meal on a spring afternoon. These are wonderful with a little salad or some new potatoes.

MAKES 8–12

- 200G/7OZ YOUNG SPINACH LEAVES, WASHED
- 100G/3½OZ/7 TBSP UNSALTED BUTTER, MELTED, PLUS 25G/1OZ/2 TBSP AND EXTRA FOR GREASING
- 50G/1¾OZ PARMESAN CHEESE, GRATED
- PINCH OF GRATED NUTMEG
- 100G/3½OZ/SCANT ½ CUP RICOTTA CHEESE
- 50G/1¾OZ/6 TBSP PINE NUTS, TOASTED
- SALT AND FRESHLY GROUND BLACK PEPPER
- 275G PACK OF FILO PASTRY

1. Heat a saucepan, add the spinach and 25g/1oz/2 tbsp butter, turn the heat to low and cover. Cook for 1 minute, then drain the spinach, pressing out as much water as you can with kitchen towel.

2. Chop the spinach, pop it in a bowl and add the Parmesan, nutmeg, ricotta and pine nuts. Stir and season to taste.

3. Preheat the oven to 220°C/425°F/gas mark 7. Grease a large baking sheet.

4. Spread 1 sheet of filo pastry on your work surface. Cover the rest with a damp tea towel to prevent it from drying out. Cut the filo sheet into 6 pieces, brush all over with the melted butter and then place 3 pieces on top of each other, turning each piece at an angle, so you end up with a star shape.

5. Spoon 1 heaped tsp of the spinach mixture onto the filo pastry, then pinch all the edges together in a parcel. Lightly brush the outside with melted butter. Repeat until you have used all the filo.

6. Put the filo parcels on the baking sheet and bake for 10 minutes, until golden and crisp. Serve with your favourite dipping sauce for a picnic.

Hot cross buns

◆◆◆

Every Easter I always looked forward to two things as a child: getting a bag of 2-pence coins from my nana and granda to play the machines at the amusement arcade, and the sweet smell when we got home for tea. Cinnamon to me was like perfume, and even now the scent takes me back to my childhood and a hot cross bun with butter.

MAKES 12

- 600G/1LB 5 OZ/5 CUPS STRONG WHITE BREAD FLOUR
- PINCH OF SALT
- 1 TSP GROUND MIXED SPICE (PUMPKIN PIE SPICE)
- 1 TSP GROUND CINNAMON
- 40G/1½OZ/3 TBSP UNSALTED BUTTER, AT ROOM TEMPERATURE, CUBED, PLUS EXTRA FOR GREASING
- 85G/3OZ/SCANT ½ CUP CASTER (SUPERFINE) SUGAR
- 150G/5½OZ/SCANT 1 CUP SULTANAS (GOLDEN RAISINS)
- 1½ TSP DRIED YEAST
- 1 EGG
- 250ML/9FL OZ/GENEROUS 1 CUP MILK, SLIGHTLY WARMED

TOPPING

- 1 TBSP PLAIN (ALL-PURPOSE) FLOUR
- 1 TBSP APRICOT JAM
- 1 TBSP GOLDEN SYRUP (LIGHT CORN SYRUP)

1. Put the flour, salt and ground spices in a bowl. Add the butter and mix until it is incorporated. Make a well in the centre and add the sugar, sultanas and yeast. Mix the egg and milk together. Slowly pour the warm liquid over the dry ingredients and knead for 5 minutes to form a soft dough.

2. Cover the bowl with cling film and leave somewhere warm and draught-free to rise for 1 hour. Lightly grease a baking sheet.

3. When the dough has doubled in volume, tip it onto a clean surface and knock it back by punching the air out of it. Shape into a ball and put it back in the bowl, cover and leave to rise for an additional 30 minutes. (My nana said proving times were a godsend as she got the housework done and prepared food for the main meal.)

4. Turn the dough out, cut it into 12 pieces and roll each into a ball. Put them on the baking sheet, cover with a tea towel, put the whole thing in a plastic bag (yes, the baking sheet, too), tie the bag and set aside somewhere warm for another 30 minutes while you make the topping.

5. Preheat the oven to 200°C/400°F/gas mark 6. To make the crosses for the topping, mix the flour with 1–2 tbsp water to form a smooth paste. Fill a piping bag with this paste. Pipe a cross on each bun. Melt the apricot jam and syrup together in a saucepan and brush lightly over the buns. Bake for 10-15minutes, or until golden brown.

6. Cool on a wire rack and serve with best butter. They'll keep for 2 days in an airtight container.

Quiche Lorraine

The ultimate quiche: smoked salty bacon, soft sweet leeks and a rich cream sauce topped with good Cheddar cheese. This is a dish I have eaten, unchanged, for the best part of 30 years. It is a wonderful teatime treat with some dressed rocket. The addition of mustard is a real winner.

MAKES 1 X 23CM/9IN QUICHE

- 1 TBSP VEGETABLE OIL
- 15G/½OZ/1 TBSP BUTTER
- 1 LEEK, SLICED
- 6 RASHERS OF SMOKED STREAKY BACON
- 2 EGGS, PLUS 2 YOLKS
- 150ML/5FL OZ/⅔ CUP DOUBLE CREAM
- 150ML/5FL OZ/⅔ CUP WHOLE MILK
- 150G/5½OZ CHEDDAR CHEESE, GRATED, PLUS EXTRA FOR SPRINKLING
- 1 TSP WHOLEGRAIN MUSTARD
- 1 X 23CM/9IN BLIND-BAKED SHORTCRUST PASTRY CASE (PAGE 17, BUT OMIT THE SUGAR)

1. Preheat the oven to 190°C/375°F/gas mark 5. Heat the oil in a frying pan, add the butter and then the leek. Cover the pan and cook over a low-medium heat for 10 minutes, until the leek is soft but not coloured. Transfer to a plate and leave to cool slightly. Cook the bacon over a medium heat for 5-6 minutes in the same pan, then remove it and chop it into small pieces.

2. In a large bowl, whisk together the eggs and yolks, then add the cream and milk and whisk. Stir in the cheese and mustard, followed by the bacon and leeks. That's your mixing done, nice and simple, as my nana used to say: 'No time for messing about, I've got 6 kids and a husband to feed.'

3. Pour the mixture into the pastry case, sprinkle with a little more cheese and bake for 30 minutes, until puffed up and golden. Leave to cool slightly and eat warm, or leave until cold, then store in the fridge for up to 4 days and eat cold.

Hello, Summer!

◆◆◆◆◆◆◆◆◆◆◆◆◆◆◆◆◆◆◆◆◆◆◆◆◆

Summertime is a real baker's delight, with
an abundance of fresh fruit in season. Summer
at my bakery is when we slip into party mode –
there's always a barbecue or birthday to
bake for. It's also the time I prepare for winter
by stashing berries in the deep freeze: they
freeze perfectly and are a godsend for the colder
months. When I was a child we spent every day
of the summer holidays on Roker Beach
on England's north-east coast. We got
a boiled egg – which was always covered in
sand – a bag of chips and £1 to play with in the
amusement arcade. Brilliant memories.

◆◆◆◆◆◆◆◆◆◆◆◆◆◆◆◆◆◆◆◆◆◆◆◆◆

The Beehive chocolate cake with raspberries

◆━◆

This is always a winner for birthdays: a perfect, light and moist chocolate cake with raspberries and added sparkle.

MAKES 1 X 20CM/8IN ROUND CAKE

- 250G/9OZ DARK CHOCOLATE (70% COCOA SOLIDS), BROKEN INTO PIECES
- 175G/6OZ/¾ CUP UNSALTED BUTTER, AT ROOM TEMPERATURE, PLUS EXTRA FOR GREASING
- 350G/12OZ/1¾ CUPS SOFT LIGHT BROWN SUGAR
- 4 EGGS
- 375G/13OZ/3 CUPS PLAIN (ALL-PURPOSE) FLOUR
- 2 TSP VANILLA EXTRACT
- 50G/1¾OZ COCOA POWDER
- 1½ TSP BAKING POWDER
- 1½ TSP BICARBONATE OF SODA (BAKING SODA)
- 400ML/14FL OZ/SCANT 1¾ CUPS MILK

CHOCOLATE BUTTERCREAM

- 175G/6OZ DARK CHOCOLATE (70% COCOA SOLIDS), BROKEN INTO PIECES
- 225G/8OZ/1 CUP UNSALTED BUTTER, AT ROOM TEMPERATURE, CUBED
- 1 TSP MILK
- 1 TSP VEGETABLE OIL
- 280G/10OZ/SCANT 2½ CUPS ICING (CONFECTIONERS') SUGAR

TOPPING

- HANDFUL OF RASPBERRIES
- EDIBLE GLITTER

1. Preheat the oven to 180°C/350°F/gas mark 4. Grease 2 x 20cm/8in diameter round cake tins and line with baking parchment.

2. Melt the chocolate in a large heatproof bowl over a pan of simmering water, making sure the bottom of the bowl doesn't touch the water.

3. Beat the butter for a minute or so, until light and fluffy. Add the sugar and beat until incorporated. Scrape down the bowl. Beat in the eggs, one at a time, adding 1 tbsp flour between each egg to keep the mixture smooth. Mix in the melted chocolate and vanilla.

4. Sift together the remaining flour, the cocoa, baking powder and bicarbonate of soda. Add a third of the flour mixture to the cake batter and beat in gently. Then add around a third of the milk, then more flour, stirring gently after each addition. Repeat with the remaining milk and flour, until all the ingredients are incorporated. Don't overbeat as this will make the cake heavy; just stir gently and stop as soon as the flour and milk are incorporated – your cake batter is done. Scrape the bowl down, then give the mixture a last stir. Spoon into the tins and level the tops.

5. Bake for 45 minutes to 1 hour, until a small knife or skewer comes out clean. Leave to cool for 10 minutes, then turn out onto a wire rack and leave to cool completely. Slice one cake in half horizontally so you have 3 layers.

6. To make the buttercream, melt the chocolate as described in step 2. Beat the butter, then add the rest of the ingredients, including the chocolate, and beat until thick and creamy. Don't overbeat or the mixture may become too hard; it should be soft and needs to be used immediately.

7. Place one of the thin cake layers on a board and spread with a quarter of the buttercream. Put the thick cake on top and spread with more buttercream, then top with the other thin cake. Crumb-coat the cake (see page 14) and leave to set for 10 minutes. Using a palette knife, spread the remaining buttercream over the top and sides of the cake. Top with raspberries and a sprinkling of glitter. This will keep in an airtight container for up to 4 days.

White forest gâteau

◆◆

This is my twist on the Black Forest Gateau: a light Génoise sponge, filled with cream, decorated with white chocolate shards and topped with a cherry compote. The compote is the recipe I used for the invention test in MasterChef, which I served with a chocolate mousse and shortbread biscuits.

MAKES 1 X 20CM/8IN ROUND CAKE

GÉNOISE SPONGE

- 250G/9OZ/1¼ CUPS CASTER (SUPERFINE) SUGAR
- 8 EGGS
- 100G/3½OZ/7 TBSP UNSALTED BUTTER, PLUS EXTRA FOR GREASING
- 250G/9OZ/2 CUPS PLAIN (ALL-PURPOSE) FLOUR

CHERRY COMPOTE

- 700G/1LB 9OZ CHERRIES, PITTED
- 100G/3½OZ/½ CUP CASTER (SUPERFINE) SUGAR
- 3 TBSP KIRSCH

FILLING AND DECORATION

- 200G/7OZ WHITE CHOCOLATE, BROKEN INTO PIECES
- 600ML/20FL OZ/2½ CUPS DOUBLE CREAM
- 1 TBSP CASTER (SUPERFINE) SUGAR
- 50G/1¾OZ/7 TBSP PISTACHIOS, TOASTED AND FINELY CHOPPED

1. To make the sponge, follow the recipe for 'The Jules' raspberry, rose and vanilla cake (page 78).

2. To make the compote, put the cherries into a pan, sprinkle over the sugar and cook over a low heat until they start to break down and release their juices. Add the kirsch and warm through for a minute. Taste and add a little more sugar if you like. Drain the cherries, reserving the juice.

3. For the decoration, melt the chocolate in a heatproof bowl over a pan of simmering water, making sure the bottom of the bowl doesn't touch the water. Remove from the heat and put 1 heaped tbsp melted chocolate on a large sheet of baking parchment. Using the back of the spoon, quickly swipe the chocolate into a long line on the paper. Repeat at least 12 times. Leave to set.

4. To assemble the cake, whip the cream with the sugar until stiff. Drizzle the reserved cherry juice over the 4 sponges. Spread about one-third of the whipped cream over one of the sponge cakes. Place another cake on top, and add more cream. Repeat, then finish with the last piece of sponge. Press gently, so the cream is pushed out of the sides of the gâteau.

5. Remove the chocolate shards from the paper and press gently around the cake. Top with the cherry compote and any remaining juices and sprinkle over the pistachios.

Banana chocolate baked Alaska

◆◆◆

This is a simple dessert to make, and includes the fastest banana ice cream ever. I love all the textures: the soft sponge, the meringue with its crisp coating and the cold ice cream. Using shop-bought sponge is fine, but if you have some time on your hands it's always best to make your own. This needs to be eaten as soon as it's ready.

MAKES 1 X 20CM/8IN ROUND CAKE

◆ ½ QUANTITY BAKED BEEHIVE CLASSIC CHOCOLATE CAKE (PAGE 123)

BANANA ICE CREAM

◆ 6 BANANAS, CUT INTO CHUNKS
◆ 25G/1OZ/2 TBSP CASTER (SUPERFINE) SUGAR
◆ 100ML/3½FL OZ/6–7 TBSP DOUBLE CREAM
◆ 100ML/3½FL OZ/6–7 TBSP BUTTERMILK OR NATURAL YOGURT

CHOCOLATE SAUCE

◆ 250ML/9FL OZ/GENEROUS 1 CUP DOUBLE CREAM
◆ 300G/10½OZ DARK CHOCOLATE (70% COCOA SOLIDS), BROKEN INTO PIECES

ITALIAN MERINGUE

◆ 175G/6OZ/GENEROUS ¾ CUP CASTER (SUPERFINE) SUGAR
◆ 3 EGG WHITES

FLAMBÉING
For a party piece try flambéing the Alaska: gently warm a ladleful of Cognac, set it alight and pour over the Alaska at the table.

1. To make the banana ice cream, put the bananas on a tray in a single layer and freeze for 1–2 hours, or until solid. Line a 18cm/6in diameter bowl with cling film.

2. Put the frozen bananas in a food processor with the sugar and a little of the cream and a little of the buttermilk. Whizz, pouring in the remaining cream and buttermilk in a steady stream. The frozen bananas will instantly freeze the liquid. Once smooth, transfer to the lined bowl and smooth the top. Cover with cling film and return to the freezer for 30 minutes, until firm. This can be made 1–2 days in advance.

3. To make the chocolate sauce, pour the cream into a small pan and place over a low heat until warm. Add the chocolate and stir constantly until it has melted.

4. Slice the chocolate sponge in half horizontally and place one half on a serving plate.

5. To make the meringue, put the sugar in a small saucepan with 6–7 tbsp water and bring to the boil. Boil for 4 minutes, until big white bubbles form and the colour just begins to change. Turn off the heat. Whip the egg whites in a large, clean glass bowl until soft peaks form, then very slowly begin to trickle the slightly cooled sugar syrup onto the egg whites, whisking continuously. Once all the syrup is incorporated, whisk to stiff peaks. The meringue should be glossy and thick.

6. Turn out the ice cream on top of the sponge. Place the other half-sponge over the ice cream and pinch the bottom and top sponges together up around the sides. Don't worry about it being perfectly neat. Using a palette knife or spatula, spread the meringue all over the sponge, making lots of rough edges and pointy bits.

7. Blast with a blowtorch. Serve with the chocolate sauce.

Baked vanilla cheesecake

◆◆

There's a lot of fear around a baked cheesecake – in particular about the possibility of the dreaded sinking middle. Don't worry if this happens; it's because it's cooled too quickly (which happens to me sometimes as I'm so impatient). Relax, fill the crater with fruit and enjoy your efforts. This is a labour of love, you can't make it and eat it on the same day unless you're up at 5am, which I've done. The crème fraîche is important, as it will make the cheesecake incredibly light. This cheesecake is cooked in a water bath, sometimes referred to as a bain-marie, in order to regulate the temperature. If the eggs are cooked at too high a heat they will scramble, and no one wants a scrambled egg cheesecake.

MAKES 1 X 20CM/8IN ROUND CAKE

◆ 150G/5½OZ/GENEROUS ½ CUP
  UNSALTED BUTTER
◆ 300G/10½OZ DIGESTIVE BISCUITS
  (GRAHAM CRACKERS), SMASHED TO
  FINE CRUMBS
◆ SEEDS SCRAPED FROM 1 VANILLA POD
◆ 800G/1LB 12OZ/3½ CUPS FULL-FAT
  SOFT CHEESE, AT ROOM TEMPERATURE
◆ 200G/7OZ/1 CUP CASTER
  (SUPERFINE) SUGAR
◆ 2 EGGS, PLUS 2 YOLKS
◆ 100ML/3½FL OZ/6–7 TBSP
  CRÈME FRAÎCHE

TOPPING

◆ 200G/7OZ RASPBERRIES
◆ 1–2 TBSP ICING
  (CONFECTIONERS') SUGAR

1. Lightly grease the bottom of a 20cm/8in round springform or loose-bottomed cake tin and line with baking parchment.

2. Melt the butter in a pan, add the biscuit crumbs and stir together until the mixture resembles wet sand. Press the crumbs firmly into the tin. Put in the fridge to set for around 10 minutes.

3. Preheat the oven to 180°C/350°F/gas mark 4. Put the vanilla seeds in a large bowl. Add the soft cheese and sugar and beat using an electric hand whisk, or a wooden spoon if your arms are up for a workout. Add the eggs and yolks, one at a time, giving everything a good mix after each addition. Finally, beat in the crème fraîche until smooth. Pour over the chilled base and smooth the top.

4. For your water bath you'll need a large, deep roasting pan. Place a couple of sheets of foil on your work surface and put your cheesecake on top. Scrunch the foil up and around the cheesecake and wrap it completely: you need to make it watertight. Put the cheesecake into the roasting pan, then pour freshly boiled water into the pan around it.

5. Carefully lift into the oven, bake for 10 minutes, and then turn the oven down to 140°C/275°F/gas mark 1 and cook for another 40 minutes, until the cheesecake is set, with a slight wobble in the middle.

6. Now's the hard part, leaving it alone! Turn the oven off, leave the door ajar and let the cheesecake cool in the oven for 1 hour or so. Letting the cake cool gradually in the oven will prevent cracks and keep it nice and light and smooth.

RECIPE CONTINUES OVERLEAF

VANILLA PODS
Also known as vanilla beans, they contain a fragrant, moist mass of tiny seeds, and it is these that you see as little black specks in good vanilla ice cream. To get at the seeds, slit the pod lengthwise with a small sharp knife and scrape out the seeds. Don't throw the vanilla pod away; pop it in a bag of caster sugar to infuse and make vanilla sugar.

RECIPE CONTINUES FROM PREVIOUS PAGE

7. When cool, remove from the oven and chill thoroughly in the fridge for at least 6 hours.

8. To make the topping, whizz three-quarters of the raspberries with the icing sugar; taste to check the sweetness. If you don't have a blender, smash the raspberries with a fork. Drizzle the topping over the cheesecake, allowing it to flow down the sides. Decorate with the remaining raspberries, or whatever fruit you like. If you feel like pushing the boat out, a little melted chocolate or edible glitter over the top would be amazing.

Lemon meringue pie cake

I adore lemon meringue pie, so I decided to put my modern twist on it. Here, the classic pie is transformed into a showstopping cake.

MAKES 1 X 20CM/8IN ROUND CAKE

- ◆ 375G/13OZ ALL-BUTTER PUFF PASTRY
- ◆ PLAIN (ALL-PURPOSE) FLOUR, FOR DUSTING

VICTORIA SPONGE

- ◆ 225G/8OZ/1 CUP UNSALTED BUTTER, CUBED, AT ROOM TEMPERATURE
- ◆ 225G/8OZ/GENEROUS 1 CUP CASTER (SUPERFINE) SUGAR
- ◆ 4 EGGS, BEATEN
- ◆ 200G/7OZ/GENEROUS 1½ CUPS SELF-RAISING FLOUR
- ◆ 1 TSP VANILLA EXTRACT
- ◆ 25G/1OZ CORNFLOUR (CORNSTARCH)

LEMON CURD

- ◆ 100G/3½OZ/½ CUP CASTER (SUPERFINE) SUGAR
- ◆ 7 TBSP CORNFLOUR (CORNSTARCH)
- ◆ GRATED ZEST AND JUICE OF 4 UNWAXED LEMONS
- ◆ 5 EGG YOLKS
- ◆ 100G/3½OZ/7 TBSP UNSALTED BUTTER, MELTED

MERINGUE

- ◆ 6 EGG WHITES
- ◆ 300G/10½OZ/1½ CUPS CASTER (SUPERFINE) SUGAR
- ◆ 1 TSP VANILLA EXTRACT

1. To make the sponge, follow the recipe for Victoria sponge (see page 81). When cool, cut horizontally into 4 thin layers.

2. Preheat the oven to 200°C/400°F/gas mark 6. Line a baking sheet with baking parchment.

3. On a lightly floured surface, roll out the pastry to around 5mm/¼in thick. Using the bottom of a 20cm/8in round cake tin as a guide, cut out 2 circles. Place the pastry on the baking sheet, cover with another piece of parchment, then put another baking sheet on top. This keeps the pastry flat and crisp. Bake for 20 minutes, until golden and crisp. Remove the top baking sheet and parchment and leave the pastry to cool.

4. To make the lemon curd, mix together the sugar, cornflour and 6–7 tbsp water. Put an additional 4 tbsp water and the lemon zest in a saucepan and bring to the boil. Slowly pour the hot liquid onto the sugar-and-cornflour mixture, whisking continuously until smooth. Quickly beat in the egg yolks and then the lemon juice. Return to the pan and whisk in the butter. Cook over a low heat, stirring continuously, until thick and glossy. Transfer to a bowl, cover and cool in the fridge.

5. To make the meringue, place a large heatproof bowl over a large pan of simmering water, making sure the bottom of the bowl doesn't touch the water. Add the egg whites and sugar to the bowl and beat with an electric hand whisk for 6 minutes, or until stiff peaks form. Remove from the heat, add the vanilla, and give it a final few seconds of beating. It will be thick and shiny and must be used right away.

6. To assemble, dab a spoonful of meringue on the serving plate and place a piece of cake on top so that it sticks to the plate. Spread with a thin layer of lemon curd, then add a layer of pastry, then curd, more cake, curd, cake, curd, cake. Top with the second pastry circle. Cover the whole stack in the meringue, using a spatula or palette knife. You can use a piping bag and nozzle to get high points on the top if you like. Blast with a blowtorch if you wish, for a golden burnished crust.

Gin and tonic dessert

◆◆◆

Here it is: the dish that got me kicked out of MasterChef. After I've eaten I enjoy refreshing, light desserts, and I thought if I could recreate the sensation of a gin and tonic but add a mousse for sweetness and a biscuit for texture I'd have a winning combination. It didn't quite work out on the day, though. I forgot to put the tonic in the jelly and the sorbet melted under the studio lights!

SERVES 4

GIN JELLY

◆ 2 SHEETS OF LEAF GELATINE
◆ 200ML/7FL OZ/GENEROUS ¾ CUP TONIC WATER
◆ 3 TBSP GIN

LEMON SORBET

◆ 175G/6OZ/GENEROUS ¾ CUP CASTER (SUPERFINE) SUGAR
◆ 20G/¾OZ GLUCOSE SYRUP
◆ 175ML/6FL OZ/¾ CUP LEMON JUICE

WHITE CHOCOLATE MOUSSE

◆ 200ML/7FL OZ/GENEROUS ¾ CUP DOUBLE CREAM
◆ 100G/3½OZ WHITE CHOCOLATE
◆ 2 EGG WHITES
◆ 40G/1½OZ/3 TBSP CASTER (SUPERFINE) SUGAR

LEMON BISCUITS

◆ 50G/1¾OZ/7 TBSP PLAIN (ALL-PURPOSE) FLOUR, PLUS EXTRA FOR DUSTING
◆ 35G/1¼OZ/2½ TBSP UNSALTED BUTTER, COLD AND CUBED, PLUS EXTRA FOR GREASING
◆ 50G/1¾OZ/¼ CUP CASTER (SUPERFINE) SUGAR
◆ GRATED ZEST OF ½ UNWAXED LEMON
◆ 1 EGG YOLK

1. First make the jelly. Soak the gelatine in a small bowl in a little cold water for a few minutes, until softened. Heat the tonic in a pan over a low heat, add the softened gelatine and stir until it has melted. Remove from the heat and stir in the gin. Pour into 4 ramekins or small martini glasses and chill until set.

2. For the sorbet, put 100ml/3½fl oz water and the sugar and glucose syrup in a pan over a medium heat and stir until the sugar has dissolved. Boil for 2 minutes, then turn the heat off and leave to cool. Measure out 175ml/6fl oz. Mix the stock syrup with the lemon juice and churn in an ice-cream machine according to the manufacturer's instructions. (Alternatively, to churn by hand, freeze the liquid in a sealable plastic container; after about an hour, break up the crystals by beating with a fork for a few seconds, then return to the freezer. Repeat every hour until frozen almost solid. This will take around 6 hours.)

3. To make the mousse, bring the cream to the boil in a pan. Remove from the heat and stir in the chocolate until melted. Leave to cool, then chill in the fridge for 30 minutes. Whip the egg whites in a clean, glass bowl until soft peaks form, then gradually add the sugar and whisk again until thick and glossy. Fold the egg whites into the cold chocolate mixture, transfer to a bowl, cover with cling film and chill until set. If the mousse isn't set enough when you are ready to serve, you can whisk the chilled mixture and it will thicken.

4. To make the biscuits, preheat the oven to 180°C/350°F/ gas mark 4. Lightly grease a baking sheet. Put the flour, butter, sugar and lemon zest in a food processor and pulse until it resembles breadcrumbs. Add the egg yolk and pulse briefly to bind the mixture. Wrap in cling film and chill in the fridge for about 15 minutes. Roll out thinly on a floured surface, cut into long rectangles and use a palette knife to lift them onto the baking sheet (the dough is very soft). Bake for about 10 minutes, until golden and crisp. Cool on a wire rack.

5. Serve the jelly with a scoop of the sorbet, a ball of the mousse scooped out with 2 spoons, and a biscuit.

Tony's cannoli

Any Sopranos fan will be familiar with these Italian pastries packed with sweetened ricotta. You can pick up cannoli tubes in most cake-supply stores and they can be used over and over again.

MAKES 8

CANNOLI TUBES

- 250G/9OZ/2 CUPS PLAIN (ALL-PURPOSE) FLOUR, PLUS EXTRA FOR DUSTING
- 1 TBSP CASTER (SUPERFINE) SUGAR
- ½ TSP GROUND CINNAMON
- PINCH OF SALT
- 3 TBSP VEGETABLE OIL, PLUS EXTRA FOR GREASING
- 125ML/4FL OZ/½ CUP DRY WHITE WINE
- 1 EGG WHITE, BEATEN
- VEGETABLE OIL, FOR DEEP-FRYING

RICOTTA FILLING

- 500G/1LB 2OZ/2 CUPS RICOTTA CHEESE
- 100G/3½OZ/¾ CUP ICING (CONFECTIONERS') SUGAR, PLUS EXTRA FOR DUSTING
- 1 TSP VANILLA EXTRACT
- ½ TSP GROUND CINNAMON
- 50G/1¾OZ HAZELNUTS, TOASTED AND FINELY CHOPPED (OPTIONAL)
- 50G/1¾OZ CHOCOLATE CHIPS (OPTIONAL)

1. Start the filling a day in advance. Scoop the ricotta into a sieve or colander, cover with cling film, then put a plate on top and weight it with a few cans of beans. Put the colander in a bowl to catch the liquid and refrigerate overnight.

2. To make the cannoli tubes, sift together the flour, sugar, cinnamon and salt, then stir in the oil and enough wine to make a soft dough, a bit like pastry. Knead the dough on a lightly floured surface for 2 minutes, until smooth. Cover and leave to rest at room temperature for about 20 minutes, or up to 1 hour. Lightly grease 8 cannoli tubes with a little oil.

3. To roll the dough, cut it into 8 sections and roll each section out to a rough circle. The dough needs to be translucent, so you can see the shadow of your hand through it. Use flour to make sure it doesn't stick as you roll, but dust off any excess flour.

4. Wrap a section of dough around each tube and secure with a little beaten egg white. Don't stretch or pull the dough, just lightly press.

5. In a large, deep pan, heat the oil to 190°C/375°F, or until a little piece of the dough browns in 20 seconds.

6. Lower 4 of the dough-wrapped tubes into the hot oil and deep-fry for 2 minutes. Remove and drain on kitchen paper. Repeat with the remaining tubes. Leave to cool on a wire rack. When completely cold, the tubes should slip out of the cannoli.

7. To finish the filling, mix the ingredients together, then work in the pressed ricotta. Spoon or pipe into the cold shells, dust with icing sugar and serve.

Super-simple summer pudding

As a kid I often went fruit-picking with my mam, and there was always bread in the house, so this was pretty much a free dessert. Summer berries are bountiful for a short time each year, so make the most of them and use a good selection. It's essential that your bread is a little stale: a 2–3-day-old farmhouse loaf is perfect. Don't use packaged sliced white; it's so full of additives it doesn't go stale!

SERVES 6

- 400G/14OZ RASPBERRIES
- 400G/14OZ MIXED SUMMER BERRIES
- 150G/5½OZ/¾ CUP CASTER (SUPERFINE) SUGAR
- 1 TSP VANILLA EXTRACT
- 7 SLICES OF SLIGHTLY STALE WHITE BREAD, CRUSTS REMOVED

1. Put all the fruit and sugar into a pan and simmer until the sugar has dissolved and the fruit is releasing plenty of juices. Stir in the vanilla.

2. Dip the bread into the fruit juice, making sure each slice is soaked right through. Place the crimson-stained bread into a 850ml/1½-pint/3½-cup pudding bowl, lining the bottom and sides and setting aside a piece for the top.

3. Drain the fruit, reserving any juices for serving. Put the drained berries into the bread-lined pudding bowl. Soak the final piece of bread in the juice and press firmly on top of the pudding.

4. Put a saucer on top of the pudding and a tin of beans on top of the saucer, which will compact the pudding. Leave in the fridge overnight or for at least 6 hours.

5. Turn out onto a serving plate and serve with the reserved berry juices, and shortbread if you wish (see page 70).

Mam!

Paris-Brest blue suede choux

◆◆

Think of this as a modern eclair made for Elvis; a fancy dessert that is the epitome of classic with a twist. The French choux pastry ring is traditionally filled with a praline cream – I have adapted this into a peanut butter cream topped with caramel and a scattering of dried banana chips. The flavours and textures are a winning combination, perfect for a teatime treat when you want something more sophisticated than a slice of cake.

MAKES 4

◆ VEGETABLE OIL, FOR GREASING

CHOUX PASTRY

◆ 70G/2½OZ/GENEROUS ½ CUP PLAIN (ALL-PURPOSE) FLOUR
◆ 50G/1¾OZ/4 TBSP UNSALTED BUTTER, CUBED
◆ PINCH OF SALT
◆ 2 EGGS, LIGHTLY BEATEN
◆ ½ TSP VANILLA EXTRACT

PEANUT BUTTER CREAM

◆ 250G/9OZ/1 CUP CRUNCHY PEANUT BUTTER
◆ 70G/2½OZ/5 TBSP UNSALTED BUTTER, AT ROOM TEMPERATURE, CUBED
◆ ½ TSP VANILLA EXTRACT
◆ 125G/4½OZ/GENEROUS 1 CUP ICING (CONFECTIONER'S) SUGAR, SIFTED
◆ 75ML/5 TBSP DOUBLE CREAM

TOPPING

◆ 40G/1½OZ/3 TBSP DARK SOFT BROWN SUGAR
◆ 40G/1½OZ/3 TBSP UNSALTED BUTTER
◆ 3 TBSP DOUBLE CREAM
◆ SMALL HANDFUL OF DRIED BANANA CHIPS, ROUGHLY CHOPPED

1. To make the choux pastry, sift the flour into a bowl and set aside. Put the butter and salt in a large saucepan with 150ml/5fl oz/⅔ cup water over a low heat until the butter has melted. Bring to the boil, remove from the heat and tip in all the flour. Beat with a wooden spoon, slowly at first otherwise you'll be covered in flour, then vigorously for a few seconds, just until the dough is smooth and leaves the sides of the pan. Return to a low heat for 2 minutes to cook out the flour, stirring all the time. Transfer to a bowl and leave to cool for a few minutes.

2. Preheat the oven to 220°C/425°F/gas mark 7. Line a baking sheet with baking parchment, then very lightly oil it.

3. Beat most of the eggs and all the vanilla into the pastry, a little at a time. The dough should be smooth and glossy and plop off the spoon. Spoon the dough into a piping bag with a 2.5cm/1in nozzle (or use a disposable piping bag and snip off the corner). Pipe 8 rings, each 13cm/5in in diameter and 2.5cm/1in thick, onto the parchment. Lightly brush the tops with the reserved egg. Bake for 10 minutes.

4. Prick holes in the sides of the pastry and return to the oven for 5 minutes; this allows steam to escape and makes crisp pastry. Leave to cool on a wire rack.

5. For the cream, beat the peanut butter and butter together, add the rest of the ingredients and beat until creamy.

6. To make the topping, put the sugar and butter into a pan and melt, then boil for 1 minute. Stir in the cream, return to the boil and then turn off the heat and leave to cool slightly. The caramel will thicken a little as it cools.

7. To assemble, take one pastry ring, turn it upside-down and push the pastry in. Pipe the peanut butter cream into the cavity. Take another ring and dip the top in the topping, then place on the peanut cream. Sprinkle with banana chips. Leave to set for 30 minutes. Serve immediately.

Focaccia

This is a traditional tear-and-share bread. I make it with different toppings, sometimes as a bread for sharing, sometimes with more substantial toppings as a meal in itself. Use leftovers as bread rolls, and fill with salami and cheeses.

SERVES 8

- ½ QUANTITY WHITE BREAD DOUGH (PAGE 19)
- LEAVES FROM 4 STEMS OF FRESH ROSEMARY
- 1 GARLIC CLOVE, CRUSHED
- 3 TSP SEA SALT
- 75ML/5 TBSP OLIVE OIL, PLUS EXTRA FOR GREASING

1. Lightly oil a 33 x 20mm/13 x 8in baking tin. Using oiled fingers, press the knocked-back bread dough into the tin (there's no need to give it a second rising), getting right into the corners. Be firm: it will spring back, but just keep pushing with your fingers and it'll get there.

2. In a mortar and pestle, pound the rosemary and garlic to release the oils, add the salt and mix.

3. Scatter the dough with the rosemary, garlic and salt mixture (or your chosen topping – see below). Press your fingers into the dough to get the distinctive indentations all over, then cover with a tea towel and leave in a warm, draught-free place for an hour to rise.

4. Preheat the oven to 200°C/400°F/gas mark 6.

5. When the dough has almost doubled in size, re-press the holes into the focaccia and sprinkle over the olive oil. Bake for 25 minutes, until golden and crisp around the outsides. Tear and share at the table.

MY FAVOURITE TOPPINGS

- Sun-blush tomatoes and fresh basil
- Goat's cheese and caramelized red onions
- Red peppers and courgette, roasted until golden
- Shredded cooked chicken and pesto

Perfect pals around pizza

◆◆◆

I always impress my mates with these pizzas. I set out a load of toppings and everyone can choose their own when they arrive. It's a really nice touch if you're having people over for a party. I always have dough in the freezer and I've been known to knock up a pizza in around 10 minutes when I get in from a night out – that's quicker than a takeaway!

MAKES 4 X 20CM/8IN PIZZAS

- ◆ ½ QUANTITY WHITE BREAD DOUGH (PAGE 19)
- ◆ 8 TBSP PASSATA
- ◆ HANDFUL OF FRESH BASIL LEAVES, TORN
- ◆ 1 GARLIC CLOVE, FINELY CHOPPED
- ◆ SALT AND FRESHLY GROUND BLACK PEPPER
- ◆ PLAIN (ALL-PURPOSE) FLOUR, FOR DUSTING
- ◆ SEMOLINA FLOUR, FOR DUSTING
- ◆ 200G/7OZ MOZZARELLA CHEESE, GRATED
- ◆ HANDFUL OF CHERRY TOMATOES, HALVED
- ◆ HANDFUL OF ROCKET
- ◆ EXTRA-VIRGIN OLIVE OIL

1. Divide the dough into 4 equal pieces, each about 100g/3½oz, and set aside.

2. Mix the passata with the basil and garlic, and season to taste. Preheat the oven to its hottest temperature.

3. Mix the plain flour and semolina flour and scatter lightly over 2 baking sheets and your work surface. Roll out the dough and place on the baking sheets (I think about 20cm/8in in diameter is perfect, but if you like your pizzas a little more doughy, don't roll them as thinly).

4. Spoon the passata equally over the pizza bases, then sprinkle with a little mozzarella. Add the cherry tomatoes and the rest of the cheese. Don't stack the toppings up – keep the layers thin and even to avoid a soggy base. Bake for 10 minutes, or until golden and crisp.

5. Top with the rocket and a drizzle of oil and serve hot.

MY FAVOURITE TOPPINGS
Replace the cherry tomatoes with...
- ◆ Cubed cooked ham and sliced mushrooms
- ◆ Thinly sliced red onion and chunks of red or green pepper; and replace the mozzarella with goat's cheese
- ◆ Shredded cooked chicken and cooked sweetcorn
- ◆ Shredded roast lamb mixed with 2 tsp harissa powder or paste and a handful of olives

TIP
You only need about half the dough on page 19 for this recipe. Divide the rest into 4 pieces, approximately 100g/3½oz each, and wrap, not too tightly, in cling film. Freeze. Wrapped individually like this, the dough only takes about 20 minutes to thaw.

Autumn Almanac

◆◆◆◆◆◆◆◆◆◆◆◆◆◆◆◆◆◆◆◆◆◆◆

As we move into autumn, my tastes and baking desires change. I don't want light and pretty; I want deep and dark. I crave warming, spicy puddings that make the most of the season's bountiful apples, plums, pears and other fruits. When I was growing up, autumn was a time of apple pies and crumbles scented with cinnamon. We nicked apples from our neighbour's garden and were always out foraging for berries and nuts. My Nana Jean wouldn't dream of making a pavlova in the autumn, when summer fruits were out of season and seriously expensive. It's so nice to look back and see how we enjoyed for free whatever the land provided. We liked eating what was cheap or foraged and my memories have inspired many of these recipes.

◆◆◆◆◆◆◆◆◆◆◆◆◆◆◆◆◆◆◆◆◆◆◆

Apple and plum loaf cake

The fruit in this recipe makes for a beautifully moist loaf; apples and plums are perfect together at this time of year – or use blackberries instead of plums. I sometimes add a little crumble mixture to the top of the loaf halfway through baking; this is one of those recipes that has lots of potential variations.

MAKES 1 X 900G/2LB LOAF

- 1 LARGE COOKING APPLE, SUCH AS BRAMLEY
- FINELY GRATED ZEST AND JUICE OF 1 UNWAXED LEMON
- 4 RIPE PLUMS, QUARTERED AND PITTED
- 2 TBSP CORNFLOUR (CORNSTARCH)
- 115G/4OZ/½ CUP UNSALTED BUTTER, AT ROOM TEMPERATURE, PLUS EXTRA FOR GREASING
- 115G/4OZ/GENEROUS ½ CUP CASTER (SUPERFINE) SUGAR, PLUS EXTRA FOR DREDGING
- 2 EGGS
- 100G/3½OZ/GENEROUS ¾ CUP SELF-RAISING FLOUR, PLUS EXTRA FOR DUSTING
- 1 TSP BAKING POWDER
- 25G/1OZ/¼ CUP GROUND ALMONDS
- CUSTARD, CREAM OR HONEY, TO SERVE

1. Preheat the oven to 180°C/350°C/gas mark 4. Grease a 900g/2lb loaf tin and scatter some flour inside, tapping out the excess.

2. Peel, core and cut the apple into 1cm/½in pieces, then put them in a bowl and squeeze over the lemon juice. Add the plums to the cornflour: this will prevent them from sinking in the batter.

3. Beat the butter for a minute or so, until light and fluffy. Add the sugar and lemon zest and beat until incorporated. Scrape down the bowl to ensure all the ingredients are combined. Beat in the eggs one at a time, adding 1 tbsp flour after each egg to keep the mixture smooth.

4. Sift together the remaining flour and the baking powder, then stir in the almonds. Gently beat the dry ingredients into the butter-and-egg mixture. Scrape down the bowl to ensure everything is evenly mixed, then fold in the fruit. Spoon the mixture into the loaf tin and level the top.

5. Bake for 45 minutes, or until a knife or skewer comes out clean. Serve with custard, cream or honey for a traditional treat.

CRUMBLE TOPPING
To make a crumble topping for this loaf, rub 50g/1¾oz/4 tbsp cold cubed butter into 100g/3½oz/generous ¾ cup plain (all-purpose) flour, then stir in 25g/1oz/2 tbsp demerara sugar. Add a little ground cinnamon if you like. Sprinkle over the loaf at the end of step 4. For the simplest of puddings, use the same topping – you'll need double the quantities, at least – over fruit and bake for 30 minutes.

The red mist cake

A simple ginger cake with the volume turned up. This fiery cake includes two types of ginger, plus ginger syrup. It's light, sticky and moist, perfect for passing round on a foggy evening. I love this as a dessert with custard, too.

MAKES 1 X 20CM/8IN ROUND CAKE

- 125G/4½OZ/GENEROUS ½ CUP UNSALTED BUTTER, PLUS EXTRA FOR GREASING
- 125G/4½OZ/GENEROUS ½ CUP DARK MUSCOVADO SUGAR
- 150G/5½OZ/SCANT ½ CUP GOLDEN SYRUP (LIGHT CORN SYRUP)
- 3 PIECES OF PRESERVED GINGER, FINELY CHOPPED, PLUS 2 TBSP SYRUP FROM THE JAR
- 2 LARGE EGGS
- 250ML/9FL OZ/1 CUP MILK
- 250G/9OZ/2 CUPS SELF-RAISING FLOUR
- 1 TSP BICARBONATE OF SODA (BAKING SODA)
- 2 TSP GROUND GINGER
- 1 TSP GROUND CINNAMON

PECAN SAUCE

- 50G/1¾OZ/4 TBSP UNSALTED BUTTER
- 50G/1¾OZ/¼ CUP DARK MUSCOVADO SUGAR
- 3 TBSP BRANDY
- 100G/3½OZ/1 CUP PECANS, TOASTED AND ROUGHLY CHOPPED

1. Preheat the oven to 180°C/350°F/gas mark 4. Grease a 20cm/8in diameter cake tin and line with baking parchment.

2. In a pan over a low-medium heat, melt the butter with the sugar, syrup, preserved ginger and ginger syrup. Let it bubble away gently, stirring, to make sure nothing sticks. Whisk together the eggs and milk and set aside.

3. Sift the flour, bicarbonate of soda, ground ginger and cinnamon together.

4. Remove the pan from the heat and tip the butter mixture into the bowl of dry ingredients. Stir to combine. Mix in the eggs and milk and stir well. The mixture should be loose and smooth with no trace of flour. Spoon into the prepared tin.

5. Bake for 35–40 minutes, or until a knife or skewer comes out clean. Leave in the tin to cool slightly, then turn out.

6. To make the sauce, melt the butter and sugar together with 3 tbsp water. When melted, turn up the heat so it begins to bubble. Add the brandy and bubble for a minute or so, then remove from the heat and taste the sauce. If the flavour of brandy is still too pronounced, cook the sauce for a minute longer. Add the pecans and stir to coat.

7. Serve the cake warm with the sauce poured over, or serve the sauce in a sauceboat. This cake keeps well for up to a week in an airtight container.

Chocasheek

◆◆

My Nana Jean has been making these for decades. I wanted something luxurious as a topping and, taking inspiration from the Ritz Hotel's afternoon tea, I came up with this recipe, named by my good friend Sam Hallam-Roberts, who tested the recipes with me. This is a beautiful dinner party dessert, but it's also a staple for afternoon tea parties. It is so rich that a small square will suffice.

MAKES 1 X 20CM/8IN SQUARE TART
- ◆ VEGETABLE OIL, FOR GREASING

CORNFLAKE PRALINE BASE
- ◆ 150G/5½OZ/¾ CUP CASTER (SUPERFINE) SUGAR
- ◆ 150G/5½OZ/GENEROUS 1 CUP HAZELNUTS, TOASTED AND SKINNED
- ◆ 100G/3½OZ/3½ CUPS CORNFLAKES

CHOCOLATE TOPPING
- ◆ 300ML/10FL OZ/1¼ CUPS DOUBLE CREAM
- ◆ 100ML/3½FL OZ/6–7 TBSP WHOLE MILK
- ◆ 300G/10½OZ DARK CHOCOLATE (70% COCOA SOLIDS), BROKEN INTO SMALL PIECES
- ◆ 2 EGGS

SMASHING THE PRALINE
If you don't have a food processor, wrap the praline in a tea towel and smash it up with a rolling pin.

1. Grease a 20cm/8in square baking tin and line with baking parchment. Lightly oil a baking sheet.

2. To make the praline for the base, put the sugar in a frying pan over a medium heat until it melts and forms an amber-coloured caramel. Do not stir or it will crystallize; just swirl the pan from time to time to make sure it's caramelizing evenly. Remove from the heat and stir in the hazelnuts. Pour the mixture immediately onto the oiled baking sheet and leave for 5–10 minutes, or until set.

3. Snap off a third of the praline and set aside for the topping. Put the remaining praline in a food processor, add the cornflakes and pulse to a fine powder. Add a splash of water (no more than a few teaspoons) to bind the mixture. Press into the prepared tin and leave in the fridge while you make the topping. (You can eat the base on its own, cut into chunky fingers and dipped in chocolate or jam.)

4. To make the topping, combine the cream and milk and bring to the boil. Remove from the heat and add the chocolate, stirring until it has melted. Quickly stir in the eggs – the mixture will become glossy and smooth. Pour over the chilled base, cover and leave in the fridge to set for at least 4 hours, or overnight.

5. To serve, snap or pull off pieces of the reserved praline and scatter it over the top; this will add a beautiful nutty crunch.

Sticky toffee blondies

◆◆

If you aren't a fan of the intense chocolate hit from a brownie, try this lighter alternative. It's a kind of sticky toffee pudding bar, packed with autumnal nuts. These are the brain-child of my mother; she wanted a sticky toffee pudding she could take to work in her packed lunch. So Jules, this one's for you!

MAKES ABOUT 20 BROWNIES

◆ 100G/3½OZ/⅔ CUP DATES
◆ 3 TBSP BOILING WATER
◆ 100G/3½OZ/7 TBSP UNSALTED BUTTER, PLUS EXTRA FOR GREASING
◆ 200G/7OZ/1 CUP SOFT LIGHT BROWN SUGAR
◆ 1 EGG
◆ 100G/3½OZ/GENEROUS ¾ CUP PLAIN (ALL-PURPOSE) FLOUR
◆ 1 TSP BAKING POWDER
◆ 100G/3½OZ/1 CUP HAZELNUTS, HALVED, OR LEFT WHOLE, TOASTED

1. Preheat the oven to 180°C/350°F/gas mark 4. Grease a 20cm/8in square baking tin and line with baking parchment.

2. Put the dates in a pan with the boiling water and bring back to the boil. Blend and set aside.

3. Put the butter and sugar in another pan over a low heat. When it has melted, remove from the heat. Whisk in the egg and then fold in the date purée.

4. Sift the flour into a bowl with the baking powder, then add the nuts and stir to coat them in the flour: this will stop them from sinking in the batter. Fold the flour-and-nut mixture into the date mixture.

5. Pour into the tin and bake for around 30 minutes. It will still be soft and squidgy – you won't be able to test it with a knife – but it will firm up as it cools. Leave in the tin to cool completely. Turn out and slice into squares. If you try to cut these when warm you'll make a mess.

Treacle tart

This was a family favourite of ours in the autumn. It's simplicity itself to make. It's really sweet, but you only need a small slice. I've added black treacle to our old family recipe, as it gives the tart a darker colour and deeper flavour.

MAKES 1 X 23CM/9IN ROUND TART

- 200ML/7FL OZ/GENEROUS ¾ CUP DOUBLE CREAM
- 200G/7OZ/GENEROUS ½ CUP GOLDEN SYRUP (LIGHT CORN SYRUP)
- 40G/1½OZ/2 TBSP BLACK TREACLE (BLACKSTRAP MOLASSES)
- 70G/2½OZ/1½ CUPS WHITE BREADCRUMBS – JUST BLITZ A COUPLE OF SLICES FROM A SLIGHTLY STALE LOAF
- 2 EGGS
- JUICE OF ½ LEMON
- 1 X 23CM/9IN BLIND-BAKED SWEET PASTRY CASE (SEE PAGE 17)
- CUSTARD OR CLOTTED CREAM, TO SERVE

1. Preheat the oven to 150°C/300°F/gas mark 2.

2. Put the cream in a large bowl and add the syrup, treacle, breadcrumbs, eggs and lemon juice. Whisk together until incorporated; don't whisk too hard as you don't want the cream to thicken.

3. Pour into the pastry case and bake for 30–40 minutes, until set. Leave to stand for 5–10 minutes, then serve warm, with custard or clotted cream.

Spiced tarte Tatin

It's the job of a baker to take something good and make it great. The humble apple pie was transformed into the tarte Tatin because of a mistake by the Tatin sisters in France in the 19th century. I wanted to take this a stage further, adding fragrant spices. I've done a lot of research for this recipe, and I found variations with cardamom, cloves and even rosemary, but I feel the star anise works best: the subtle aniseed flavour lends itself beautifully to the sharp apples and the sweet caramel. I don't have a special Tatin pan – I just use a frying pan with a metal handle that I can put in the oven.

SERVE 6

- 100G/3½OZ/½ CUP CASTER (SUPERFINE) SUGAR
- 50G/1¾OZ/4 TBSP UNSALTED BUTTER, COLD AND DICED
- 2 STAR ANISE
- 1 VANILLA POD, SLIT AND SEEDS SCRAPED OUT
- 5 DESSERT APPLES, SUCH AS COX'S, PEELED, CORED AND CUT INTO QUARTERS
- UNSALTED BUTTER, MELTED, FOR BRUSHING
- 375G/13OZ ALL-BUTTER PUFF PASTRY
- CLOTTED CREAM, TO SERVE

1. Preheat the oven to 190°C/375°F/gas mark 5.

2. Put the sugar and 3 tbsp water in an ovenproof frying pan, about 20-25cm (8-10in) in diameter. Swirl to combine and place over a medium-high heat until you have a deep golden amber caramel; this will indicate the final colour of your tart. Don't stir the caramel or the sugar will crystallize, just swirl the pan from time to time to make sure that it's caramelizing evenly.

3. Remove from the heat and immediately add the butter, star anise, vanilla seeds and pod; swirl to combine.

4. Pack the apples directly on top of the caramel, nice and tight, cut-side up (the smooth peeled side will be on top when it's turned out.) Brush the apples with a little melted butter and set aside while you prepare the pastry.

5. Roll out the pastry to about 5mm/¼in thick and cut a circle slightly larger than the pan. Prick it all over with a fork and place over the apples, tucking down the sides. Brush with melted butter and bake for 30 minutes, until the pastry is risen and golden.

6. Remove the pan from the oven (be careful; the handle will be hot) and leave to stand for 5 minutes. Invert a large plate over the top of the pan and flip upside-down to release the tart. Serve hot or cold, with clotted cream. Store in the fridge for up to 5 days.

Baklava

Layers of the thinnest, crispest pastry, an abundance of toasted nuts, all sweetened with delicious honey... what's not to like? Please do try making this yourself, the difference between homemade and shop-bought is unbelievable. The origins of this delicacy are fiercely contested, but we know that the word 'baklava' was introduced to English culture in the 1600s. Imagine that: 400 years and still going strong. Whenever I'm invited for dinner in the summer this is the gift I take, a huge box of baklava, which we eat with iced lemon tea. Bliss.

MAKES ABOUT 30 PIECES

- 500G/1LB 2OZ/4 CUPS NUTS (TOASTED) (I USE A COMBINATION OF PISTACHIOS, WALNUTS, HAZELNUTS AND ALMONDS)
- 175G/6OZ/GENEROUS ¾ CUP CASTER (SUPERFINE) SUGAR
- 4 TBSP RUNNY HONEY
- 275G PACK OF FILO PASTRY
- 200G/7OZ/GENEROUS ¾ CUP UNSALTED BUTTER, MELTED, PLUS EXTRA FOR GREASING
- PISTACHIOS, FINELY GROUND, TO DECORATE (OPTIONAL)

HONEY SYRUP

- 200G/7OZ/1 CUP CASTER (SUPERFINE) SUGAR
- 175G/6OZ/½ CUP RUNNY HONEY
- JUICE OF 1 LEMON
- 2 TBSP ORANGE BLOSSOM WATER
- 1 CINNAMON STICK, OR A PINCH OF GROUND CINNAMON

1. Preheat the oven to 180°C/350°F/gas mark 4. Grease a 23cm/9in square tin and line with baking parchment.

2. Smash the nuts up in a food processor, or wrap them in a clean tea towel and smash with a rolling pin. Put them in a bowl with the sugar and honey and stir.

3. Open out the filo pastry and cover with a damp tea towel to prevent it from drying out. Place 4 sheets of filo in the bottom of the prepared tin, brushing each one liberally with butter before adding the next. Scatter the top of the fourth layer with some of the nut mixture.

4. Top with 2 more sheets of filo, again brushing each sheet liberally with butter, and sprinkle with the nut mixture. Repeat with 2 more sheets of filo and nuts. Cover with 4 sheets of filo, again liberally buttered after each layer. Cut the baklava into diamonds or small squares, using a very sharp knife. Bake for 35 minutes, or until golden.

5. To make the syrup, put all the ingredients in a pan, add 175ml/6fl oz/¾ cup water and bring to the boil. Turn the heat down and simmer for 5 minutes, or until syrupy and slightly thick. Pour evenly over the cooked baklava; if you used a cinnamon stick, remove it before pouring. Scatter with the ground pistachios.

6. Chill or leave at room temperature for at least 3 hours. The syrup will soften the pastry and make it easier to re-cut. It will keep in an airtight container for up to a week.

Hazelnut meringue and brownie layer cake

◆◆

**Instead of a sponge, try this meringue-based cake for a birthday celebration.
Its soft and chewy cake layers are lighter than sponge and the filling is a dense
fudge brownie. The slight crispness of the meringue adds another texture and the
fruit cuts through the richness. I use natural yogurt as a filling as it's not as heavy
as cream. This is lovely filled with fresh blackberries.**

MAKES 1 X 20CM/8IN ROUND CAKE

HAZELNUT MERINGUE
- ◆ VEGETABLE OIL, FOR GREASING
- ◆ 4 EGG WHITES
- ◆ 200G/7OZ/1 CUP CASTER
  (SUPERFINE) SUGAR
- ◆ 1 TSP CORNFLOUR (CORNSTARCH)
- ◆ 1 TSP WHITE-WINE VINEGAR
- ◆ 150G/5½OZ/¾ CUP
  HAZELNUTS, TOASTED, SKINNED
  AND FINELY GROUND

BROWNIE
- ◆ 150G/5½OZ/GENEROUS ½ CUP
  UNSALTED BUTTER
- ◆ 140G/5OZ DARK CHOCOLATE
  (70% COCOA SOLIDS), BROKEN
  INTO PIECES
- ◆ 55G/2OZ COCOA POWDER
- ◆ 40G/1½OZ/5 TBSP PLAIN
  (ALL-PURPOSE) FLOUR
- ◆ ¾ TSP BAKING POWDER
- ◆ 225G/8OZ/GENEROUS 1 CUP
  CASTER (SUPERFINE) SUGAR
- ◆ 3 EGGS, BEATEN

FILLING AND TOPPING
- ◆ 150G/5½OZ/GENEROUS ½ CUP
  NATURAL YOGURT
- ◆ HANDFUL OF FROZEN
  RASPBERRIES, THAWED
- ◆ ICING (CONFECTIONERS') SUGAR OR
  EDIBLE GLITTER (OPTIONAL)

1. Preheat the oven to 190°C/375°F/gas mark 5.
Lightly oil 2 x 20cm/8in diameter cake tins and line with
baking parchment.

2. To make the hazelnut meringue, whip the egg whites
in a large, clean glass bowl until soft peaks form, then whisk
in the sugar, a little at a time, until stiff peaks form. Beat in
the cornflour and vinegar, then fold in the hazelnuts. Divide
between the tins and level the tops. Bake for 35 minutes.
Turn the oven off, open the door and leave the meringues
in the oven to cool for 1 hour. When they are cold, peel
off the paper and set aside.

3. To make the brownie, preheat the oven to 180°C/350°F/
gas mark 4. Line a 20cm/8in diameter tin with baking
parchment. Melt the butter and chocolate in heatproof bowl
set over a pan of simmering water, making sure the bottom
of the bowl doesn't touch the water. Stir every 30 seconds,
until smooth.

4. In a separate bowl, sift together the cocoa, flour and
baking powder, then add the sugar. Add the dry ingredients
to the melted chocolate mixture and stir well. Add the eggs
and mix until you have a silky consistency. Pour into the tin
and bake for 25 minutes, until slightly springy to the touch.
It will still be wobbly, which is fine, but it will firm up as it
cools. Leave to cool in the tin.

5. To serve, place a round of hazelnut meringue on a plate,
smother in yogurt, then add the berries. Cover with the
brownie layer, then the second meringue. Pile more yogurt
and berries on top. You could also add a dusting of icing
sugar, or sprinkle with edible glitter.

Sticky apple pudding with brandy toffee sauce

◆◆

This is one of those Sunday afternoon desserts: rich, unctuous and screaming to be eaten in front of the fire with the telly on. Leave the sultanas out if you aren't keen, but they do add a wonderful texture.

SERVES 4–6

- 100G/3½OZ/GENEROUS ½ CUP SULTANAS (GOLDEN RAISINS)
- 3 TBSP BRANDY
- 250G/9OZ/2 CUPS PLAIN (ALL-PURPOSE) FLOUR
- 1½ TSP BICARBONATE OF SODA (BAKING SODA)
- PINCH OF SALT
- 1 TSP GROUND CINNAMON
- 1 TSP GROUND ALLSPICE
- 100G/3½OZ/½ CUP CASTER (SUPERFINE) SUGAR
- 300G/10½OZ/1½ CUPS DARK BROWN SUGAR
- 2 EGGS
- 225G/8OZ/1 CUP UNSALTED BUTTER, MELTED, PLUS EXTRA FOR GREASING
- 3 MEDIUM OR 2 LARGE COOKING APPLES, PEELED AND CUT INTO CHUNKS
- 100G/3½OZ/1 CUP NUTS, SUCH AS PECANS OR HAZELNUTS, TOASTED

BRANDY TOFFEE SAUCE

- 150G/5½OZ/GENEROUS ½ CUP UNSALTED BUTTER
- 150G/5½OZ/¾ CUP DARK BROWN SUGAR
- 300ML/10FL OZ/1¼ CUPS DOUBLE CREAM

1. Preheat the oven to 180°C/350°F/gas mark 4. Grease a 23cm/9in square cake tin and line the bottom with baking parchment.

2. Put the sultanas in a bowl and cover with the brandy. Leave for 15 minutes, then drain, reserving the brandy.

3. Sift the flour, bicarbonate of soda, salt, cinnamon and allspice into a bowl.

4. In a separate bowl, whisk together both sugars and the eggs until light and mousse-like. Add the melted butter and whisk well. Fold the dry ingredients into the egg mixture and then fold in the apples, nuts and sultanas. Spoon into the cake tin and level the top. Bake for 1 hour, or until a knife or skewer comes out clean.

5. To make the sauce, put the butter and sugar into a small pan and bring to the boil. Add the cream and warm through, then stir in the reserved brandy and remove from the heat.

6. The cake will keep for up to 5 days. Wrap it in cling film or store in an airtight container. The sauce can be reheated, but it will lose its brandy kick as the alcohol boils off.

Pecan bourbon and cinnamon sticky-sweet buns

Soft, sweet dough, scented with cinnamon and topped with bourbon-soaked pecans – aren't you dying to try these? I came up with the recipe after a particularly dull Chelsea bun. I loved the dough but craved something more exciting as a topping. These are good for all occasions, but the cinnamon always makes me think of autumn time.

MAKES 10 BUNS

DOUGH

- 215G/7½OZ/SCANT 1¾ CUPS STRONG WHITE BREAD FLOUR, PLUS EXTRA FOR DUSTING
- 215G/7½OZ/SCANT 1¾ CUPS PLAIN (ALL-PURPOSE) FLOUR
- 2 TSP CORNFLOUR (CORNSTARCH)
- 1 TSP SALT
- 165ML/5½FL OZ/SCANT ¾ CUP MILK
- 90G/3¼OZ/SCANT ½ CUP CASTER (SUPERFINE) SUGAR
- 10G/¼OZ DRIED YEAST OR 20G/¾OZ FRESH YEAST
- 2 EGGS, BEATEN
- 70G/2½OZ/5 TBSP UNSALTED BUTTER, AT ROOM TEMPERATURE, CUBED

FILLING

- 85G/3OZ/6 TBSP UNSALTED BUTTER, SOFTENED
- 1 TBSP GROUND CINNAMON
- 1 TBSP CASTER (SUPERFINE) SUGAR

BOURBON PECANS

- 300G/10½OZ/2½ CUPS PECANS
- 50G/1¾OZ/¼ CUP CASTER (SUPERFINE) SUGAR
- 50G/1¾OZ/¼ CUP SOFT LIGHT BROWN SUGAR
- 75ML/5 TBSP BOURBON
- 2 TSP VANILLA EXTRACT
- 75G/2¾OZ/5 TBSP UNSALTED BUTTER, CUBED

1. To make the dough, put all the flours and salt into a food mixer with a dough-hook attachment.

2. Warm the milk in a pan, then remove from the heat and add the sugar and yeast. Stir, then leave for a minute to activate the yeast.

3. Pour the milky mixture into the dry ingredients and begin to stir. Add the eggs – reserving about ½ an egg for the glaze – and butter and combine to a soft dough. At first the mixture will be really sticky, but it will come together as you knead, so don't be tempted to add more flour. Knead for 15 minutes to develop the gluten.

4. Cover the bowl with a tea towel or cling film and leave in a warm, draught-free place to rise for 1 hour.

5. Knock back the dough, punching the air out, cover and leave for 15 minutes to relax.

6. On a lightly floured surface, roll out the dough to a rectangle around 1cm/½in thick.

7. For the filling, spread the butter over the dough, sprinkle with the cinnamon and sugar and roll up like a Swiss roll. Slice the roll into 10 equal pieces and set aside while you prepare the pecans.

8. Sprinkle the pecans in the bottom of a 25 x 20cm/10 x 8in baking tin, then sprinkle over the sugars, bourbon and vanilla. Dot the butter all over.

9. Place the 10 slices of dough on top of the pecans, spaced apart as they will expand as they rise and cook. Cover with a tea towel or cling film and leave in a warm, draught-free place to rise for around 45 minutes.

10. Preheat the oven to 190°C/375°F/gas mark 5. Carefully brush the tops of the risen buns with the reserved beaten egg and bake for 25 minutes. You might need to cover the top with foil after 10 minutes to prevent them from from browning too much. Leave to cool slightly before turning. Tear the sweet buns apart and dive in. They are best eaten straight out of the oven and definitely within 24 hours.

Nutty toffee apples

These are so simple to make and great for the kids or guests at a Halloween or bonfire party. The nuts are optional, but I love the extra crunch: try walnuts, hazelnuts and almonds. You will need wooden lollipop sticks, which you can buy from craft stores or save from bought ice creams. I make these as gifts for trick or treaters, wrapped in cellophane.

MAKES 6

- ◆ 500G/1LB 2OZ/2½ CUPS CASTER (SUPERFINE) SUGAR
- ◆ 50G/1¾OZ/4 TBSP UNSALTED BUTTER
- ◆ VEGETABLE OIL, FOR GREASING
- ◆ 6 SHARP, CRISP APPLES
- ◆ 200G/7OZ NUTS, TOASTED, VERY FINELY CHOPPED

1. To make the caramel, put the sugar in a pan with 200ml/7fl oz/generous ¾ cup water and cook over a medium heat until you have an amber-coloured caramel. Do not stir or the sugar will crystallize; just swirl the pan occasionally to make sure it's caramelizing evenly. Add the butter and swirl to combine.

2. Lightly oil a piece of greaseproof paper. Insert the lollipop sticks in the bottom of the apples, pressing in firmly. Pat the apples dry, then dip them into the caramel, carefully as it will be very hot. Immediately scatter the toasted nuts over the toffee.

3. Stand the apples on their tops, sticks in the air, on the oiled paper and leave the caramel to harden – about 30 minutes will do it.

4. Enjoy greedily, there really is no way to eat a toffee apple gracefully!

Peanut butter fudge

◆◆

This is a wicked bonfire treat, passed round the fire with marshmallows and cocoa. It takes a mere 10 minutes to whip up. Pack it in pretty Kilner jars decorated with ribbon and personalized tags for a gift. You can substitute a third of the peanut butter for Nutella chocolate hazelnut spread to make chocolate peanut butter fudge.

MAKES ABOUT 30 PIECES

◆ 280G/10OZ/SCANT 2½ CUPS ICING (CONFECTIONERS') SUGAR

◆ 140G/5OZ/GENEROUS ½ CUP UNSALTED BUTTER, PLUS EXTRA FOR GREASING

◆ 140G/5OZ/SCANT ½ CUP GOOD-QUALITY CRUNCHY PEANUT BUTTER

◆ ½ TSP VANILLA EXTRACT

◆ 200G/7OZ/1½ CUPS SALTED PEANUTS, RUBBED VIGOROUSLY TO REMOVE MOST OF THE SALT

1. Lightly grease a 20cm/8in square tin. Sift the icing sugar into a bowl.

2. Place the butter and peanut butter in a saucepan over a medium heat until the mixture comes to a boil. Remove from the heat. Add the vanilla, then pour the mixture over the icing sugar and stir with a wooden spoon until smooth, with no traces of icing sugar.

3. Pour the mixture into the prepared tin, scatter with the peanuts, pressing them in slightly, and place in the fridge to set for about 1 hour.

4. Turn the fudge out of the tin and cut into pieces using a hot, sharp knife.

Rose marshmallows

◆◆

What bonfire party would be complete without marshmallows toasted on whopping great sticks until burnished, golden and meltingly tender? I love the flavour of rose water, but if you don't like it just leave it out. Choose any colour you like for the marshmallows; I recommend a gel colour as they are better than liquid food colourings. Precision is everything in this recipe, so you'll need a timer.

MAKES ABOUT 5-30 PIECES

◆ 6 SHEETS OF LEAF GELATINE, ABOUT 2G EACH
◆ 125ML/4FL OZ/½ CUP ICE-COLD WATER
◆ 325G/11½OZ/GENEROUS 1½ CUPS GRANULATED SUGAR
◆ 350G/12OZ LIQUID GLUCOSE
◆ PINCH OF SALT
◆ 2 TSP VANILLA EXTRACT
◆ 4 TBSP ROSE WATER
◆ 1 TINY DROP OF PINK GEL FOOD COLOURING
◆ 40G/1½OZ/5 TBSP ICING (CONFECTIONERS') SUGAR
◆ 40G/1½OZ/5 TBSP CORNFLOUR (CORNSTARCH)
◆ VEGETABLE OIL, FOR GREASING

1. Put the gelatine and ice-cold water into the bowl of a food mixer with the paddle attachment.

2. In a small saucepan put 125ml/4fl oz/½ cup water the sugar, glucose and salt. Place over a medium heat, cover and cook for 4 minutes. Uncover and cook for a further 8 minutes. If you have a sugar thermometer it should reach 240°F/115°C, but if not, don't worry; 8 minutes will do it. You can test it by dropping a few drops of the liquid into a glass of cold water: it should form a soft, squeezable ball.

3. Remove from the heat and take the pan to your mixer. Give the gelatine a quick stir to make sure it is thoroughly softened. Turn the mixer on to a slow speed and pour the hot sugar mixture onto the gelatine. Once all the sugar is in, increase the speed to high and beat for around 15 minutes, until the mixture is really thick. Add the vanilla, rose water and colouring and beat for another minute or two.

4. Sift the icing sugar and cornflour together. Lightly oil the sides and bottom of a 20cm/8in square baking tin and coat with some of the icing-sugar mixture; tap out the excess and reserve. Pour the marshmallow mixture into the tin and dust over some of the reserved icing-sugar mixture. Leave to set, uncovered, for at least 3 hours, or overnight, at room temperature.

5. Turn the marshmallow out onto a cutting board and cut into pieces. A pizza cutter wheel makes this easy. Dust with the remaining icing-sugar mixture. (If there isn't enough, just make some more using equal quantities of icing sugar and cornflour.) Store in an airtight container for up to 2 weeks.

Pumpkin, pear and Gorgonzola flatbread

Pumpkins and pears are bountiful throughout the autumn; in this recipe the natural sweetness of both is counterbalanced with the rich saltiness of the Gorgonzola. I serve these as part of a 'pickie tea' as my mam calls it – the Italians call it antipasti. Smaller versions make a great first course topped with some dressed rocket. Unless you have a large oven that can take 3 baking sheets, you'll need to make these in 2 batches.

MAKES 6 X 20CM/8IN FLATBREADS

- 1 QUANTITY WHITE BREAD DOUGH (PAGE 19)
- PLAIN (ALL-PURPOSE) FLOUR AND SEMOLINA FLOUR, FOR DUSTING

TOPPING

- ½ PUMPKIN, PEELED AND CUT INTO CHUNKS
- 3–4 TBSP OLIVE OIL
- SALT AND FRESHLY GROUND BLACK PEPPER
- 150G/5½OZ GORGONZOLA CHEESE, CRUMBLED
- 3 RIPE PEARS, PEELED, CORED AND CUT INTO QUARTERS, THEN HALVED AGAIN
- HANDFUL OF PINE NUTS, TOASTED
- EXTRA-VIRGIN OLIVE OIL

1. Preheat the oven to 200°C/400°F/gas mark 6.

2. To make the topping, place the pumpkin on a baking sheet. Sprinkle with the olive oil, salt and pepper and roast for 30 minutes, until tender. Set aside to cool.

3. Turn the oven up to its highest setting. Scatter the flours over 3 baking sheets and your work surface.

4. Divide the dough into 6 equal pieces, each about 150g/5½oz. Roll or press out each piece into a rough circle about 20cm/8in in diameter and 5mm/¼in thick. Place on the baking sheets.

5. Top with the cheese, then scatter over the pumpkin and pears. Brush the top with a little olive oil. Bake for 9–10 minutes, or until golden and puffed up. The bases should be crisp, with a springy, doughy crust.

6. Scatter with the pine nuts and drizzle with extra-virgin olive oil. Serve warm.

Ham and cheese cookies

These make wonderful canapés and are a favourite treat of mine with a glass of red wine after a particularly hectic day. The method is similar to choux pastry. It's a little unusual but the result is crisp, light and unbelievably moreish. It's essential to sieve the flour to get a smooth dough.

MAKES 24

- 75G/2¾OZ/5 TBSP UNSALTED BUTTER, PLUS EXTRA FOR GREASING
- SALT AND FRESHLY GROUND BLACK PEPPER
- 85G/3OZ/¾ CUP PLAIN (ALL-PURPOSE) FLOUR, SIFTED
- 3 EGGS
- 70G/2½OZ GOOD-QUALITY HAM, FINELY CHOPPED
- 200G/7OZ OF YOUR FAVOURITE MELTING CHEESE, GRATED (I LOVE JARLSBERG)

1. Preheat the oven to 200°C/400°F/gas mark 6. Lightly grease a baking sheet.

2. Melt the butter in a saucepan, then add 150ml/5fl oz/generous ½ cup water and a pinch of salt and pepper. Bring to a simmer, then turn the heat to low. Add the flour and stir vigorously until the mixture comes away from the sides of the pan – it'll only take a minute. Turn off the heat and leave to cool for a few minutes.

3. Beat in the eggs a little at a time, you might not need all of them as the mixture should plop off the spoon and not be runny. Stir in the ham and cheese. Spoon the dough into a piping bag (this isn't essential; you can simply spoon the mixture onto the baking sheet, but it does look nice piped). Pipe or spoon in small balls, just over 2.5cm/1in wide and spaced well apart. Bake for 25 minutes, until golden.

4. Delicious warm, or cool on a wire rack and store in an airtight container for up to 4 days.

Welcome to Winter

◆◆◆◆◆◆◆◆◆◆◆◆◆◆◆◆◆◆◆◆◆◆◆

Winter is the classic baking season, with pies
and warming puddings – this is food that
sticks to your ribs. Winter really is a season
where you need to forget the diet, forget the
healthy eating and simply indulge. My Auntie
Jeanette always said that in winter you need
to 'warm yer puddins', which is Sunderland-
speak for 'warm your tummy'. Winter is
also the perfect time to grab your summer
fruits out of the deep freeze to brighten up
puddings or make some jam; I love a good
suet pudding, but it's also nice to have a scone
with homemade raspberry jam. Desperately
seeking the start of the warmer seasons.

◆◆◆◆◆◆◆◆◆◆◆◆◆◆◆◆◆◆◆◆◆◆◆

Beehive black cake

◆◆◆

A rich, moist cake. It's an unusual method, but trust me: you won't be disappointed. The large amount of sugar is necessary to counterbalance the bitterness of the Guinness, so don't be tempted to cut it down. The classic cream cheese frosting cuts the richness of the cake beautifully. Chocolate buttercream is also fantastic with this.

MAKES 1 X 20CM/8IN ROUND CAKE

- 250ML/9FL OZ/GENEROUS 1 CUP GUINNESS
- 400G/14OZ/2 CUPS CASTER (SUPERFINE) SUGAR
- 100G/3½OZ COCOA POWDER
- 250G/9OZ/GENEROUS 1 CUP UNSALTED BUTTER, PLUS EXTRA FOR GREASING
- 2 EGGS
- 100ML/3½FL OZ/6–7 TBSP BUTTERMILK
- 1 TSP VANILLA EXTRACT
- 250G/9OZ/2 CUPS PLAIN (ALL-PURPOSE) FLOUR
- 2 TSP BICARBONATE OF SODA (BAKING SODA)
- 1 TSP SALT

CREAM CHEESE FROSTING

- 125G/4½OZ/GENEROUS ½ CUP UNSALTED BUTTER, AT ROOM TEMPERATURE
- 175G/6OZ/¾ CUP FULL-FAT SOFT CHEESE
- 1 TSP VANILLA EXTRACT
- 500G/1LB 2OZ/4¼ CUPS ICING (CONFECTIONERS') SUGAR
- COCOA POWDER, FOR DUSTING

1. Preheat the oven to 180°C/350°F/gas mark 4. Grease a 20cm/8in diameter tin and line with baking parchment.

2. Put the Guinness, sugar, cocoa and butter in a pan over a low heat and stir gently until the butter has melted. Leave to cool slightly.

3. In a large bowl or food mixer, beat the eggs with the buttermilk and vanilla, then add the Guinness mixture, beating until combined.

4. Sift the flour, bicarbonate of soda and salt together. Add the flour mixture to the Guinness mixture in 3 stages, stirring gently after each addition. Scrape down the sides of the bowl and mix to make sure everything is evenly combined.

5. Pour the mixture into the prepared tin; it'll be really runny. Bake for 45 minutes, until a knife or skewer inserted into the cake comes out clean. Leave to cool in the tin for 10 minutes, then turn out onto a wire rack and leave to cool completely before decorating.

6. To make the frosting, beat the butter until softened. Add the soft cheese and beat gently, then add the vanilla and icing sugar and beat until thick and creamy. Spread over the top and sides of the cake and dust with cocoa.

Singin' hinnies

This is a traditional northern teatime treat. Singin' hinnies are so-called because of the whistling noise they make as they are cooking, and 'hinnie' is a northern word for 'honey' or 'child'. Like so many of my hand-me-down recipes, this is really simple and quick to make: there's no jargon, my nana just wrote down the basic instructions. Nana Jean and all my aunties and cousins can make these blindfolded, I'm sure. We eat them hot and buttered with jam, or the savoury ones fried until crisp with a full English breakfast.

MAKES 12

- 225G/8OZ/1¾ CUPS PLAIN (ALL-PURPOSE) FLOUR, PLUS EXTRA FOR DUSTING
- 1 TSP BAKING POWDER
- PINCH OF SALT
- 80G/3OZ/6 TBSP LARD, COLD AND CUBED, PLUS EXTRA FOR COOKING
- 80G/3OZ/6 TBSP UNSALTED BUTTER, COLD AND CUBED
- 100G/3½OZ CURRANTS OR SULTANAS (GOLDEN RAISINS) (OPTIONAL)
- 50G/1¾OZ/¼ CUP CASTER (SUPERFINE) SUGAR (OPTIONAL)
- MILK, TO BIND

1. Sift together the flour, baking powder and salt into a large bowl. Rub in the lard and butter (you can use all butter if you like, but lard gives a wonderful flavour). If you're making sweet singin' hinnies, mix in the currants and sugar.

2. Add milk to bind to a soft dough. The amount varies, depending on your flour, so just add a little at a time and stir until bound. Turn onto a floured surface and roll out to a circle around 2.5cm/1in thick. Cut into 12 segments, like the numbers on a clock.

3. Place a heavy-bottomed frying pan over a medium heat and add a little lard (lard has a high smoking point; olive oil isn't suitable). Cook the hinnies for 3 minutes on each side, or until pale brown and firm. Serve fresh from the pan.

Granda Ernie and friend, and brother John

Quince ricotta cheesecake with cinnamon maple glaze

◆◆◆

This is my favourite cheesecake of all time. Ricotta gives a lighter texture than cream cheese. Quince is a member of the apple and pear family: fragrant, golden yellow and in season from late autumn through the winter months. If you can't find quinces, use apples or pears instead. In summer you could use ripe nectarines – there's no need to soften them first.

MAKES 1 X 20CM/8IN ROUND CAKE

◆ 150G/5½OZ/¾ CUP UNSALTED BUTTER, PLUS EXTRA FOR GREASING
◆ 300G/10½OZ DIGESTIVE BISCUITS (GRAHAM CRACKERS), SMASHED TO FINE CRUMBS

FILLING

◆ 3 QUINCES
◆ 40G/1½OZ/3 TBSP UNSALTED BUTTER
◆ 200G/7OZ/1 CUP CASTER (SUPERFINE) SUGAR
◆ 5 TBSP SOFT LIGHT BROWN SUGAR
◆ 800G/1LB 12OZ/3¼ CUPS RICOTTA CHEESE
◆ 35G/1¼OZ/4 TBSP PLAIN (ALL-PURPOSE) FLOUR
◆ SEEDS SCRAPED FROM 1 VANILLA POD
◆ 3 EGGS

TOPPING

◆ ½ TSP GROUND CINNAMON
◆ 3 TBSP MAPLE SYRUP

1. Lightly grease a 20cm/8in round springform or loose-bottomed cake tin and line with baking parchment. Melt the butter in a pan. Remove from the heat, add the biscuit crumbs and stir until it resembles wet sand. Press the crumbs firmly into the prepared tin to make an even layer. Put into the fridge to set for around 10 minutes. Preheat the oven to 170°C/325°F/gas mark 3.

2. To make the filling, peel and core 2 quinces and cut them into chunks. Melt the butter in a pan, add the chopped quinces, sprinkle over 3 tbsp caster sugar and 3 tbsp brown sugar and cook, uncovered, for a minute to soften the fruits slightly. Set aside.

3. Put the ricotta, remaining caster sugar, flour and vanilla seeds in a large bowl and beat until combined. Add the eggs, one at a time, beating after each addition so the mixture stays smooth.

4. Using a slotted spoon, scoop out the cooked quinces and pat dry. Discard the cooking liquid. Add the quinces to the ricotta mixture and gently fold in. Spoon the mixture over the chilled biscuit base.

5. Peel and core the remaining quince and slice thinly. Arrange over the cheesecake and scatter with the remaining 2 tbsp brown sugar. Bake for 1–1¼ hours. The cheesecake should be set with a slight wobble in the middle and a knife should come out clean.

6. Leave in the tin to cool completely, then unmould and transfer to the fridge to chill. To serve, mix the cinnamon with the maple syrup and drizzle over the cheesecake.

Apple Charlotte

This is incredibly simple to make and a real winner with my family. I serve it with a light vanilla custard. It's important to use good white bread, such as a farmhouse loaf. It's essential the bread is a little stale – 48 hours old is perfect.

SERVES 4–6

- ◆ 900G/2LB BRAMLEY OR OTHER COOKING APPLES, PEELED, CORED AND ROUGHLY CHOPPED
- ◆ GRATED ZEST AND JUICE OF 1 UNWAXED LEMON
- ◆ 50G/1¾OZ/¼ CUP SOFT LIGHT BROWN SUGAR
- ◆ 1 TSP GROUND CINNAMON
- ◆ 85G/3OZ/6 TBSP UNSALTED BUTTER, MELTED
- ◆ 4–6 SLICES OF WHITE BREAD FROM A FARMHOUSE LOAF, 2–3 DAYS OLD, CRUSTS REMOVED

LIGHT VANILLA CUSTARD

- ◆ 150ML/5FL OZ/⅔ CUP MILK
- ◆ 1 VANILLA POD, SLIT LENGTHWAYS
- ◆ 4 EGG YOLKS
- ◆ 50G/1¾OZ/¼ CUP CASTER (SUPERFINE) SUGAR

1. Put the apples in a saucepan with the lemon zest and juice, sugar and cinnamon and cook over a low heat, uncovered, until broken down and bubbling, stirring occasionally. Give it a good beat to make sure it's smooth, and then set aside.

2. Preheat the oven to 190°C/375°F/gas mark 5. Grease a 900g/2lb pudding bowl or a 15cm/6in diameter deep cake tin with a little of the melted butter. Use the rest of the butter to brush the bread on one side. Line the bowl or tin with the bread, buttered-side pressed against the buttered dish, overlapping as you go. Press the bread all round the bottom and sides, making sure there are no gaps.

3. Fill the cavity with the apple purée, then cover the purée with more bread and press together with the bread around the sides to seal the Charlotte. Press down firmly; if I'm not baking the Charlotte straight away I'll put a plate over it and weigh it down with a tin of beans. Bake for 30 minutes, until golden and crisp.

4. To make the custard, warm the milk with the vanilla pod, then turn off the heat and leave to infuse for 5–10 minutes. Meanwhile, beat the egg yolks and sugar together for 5 minutes, until light and mousse-like.

5. Slowly pour the warm infused milk over the eggs and sugar, whisking all the time to make sure the eggs don't scramble. Return to the pan, scoop out the vanilla pod and cook over a low heat for a few minutes, stirring all the time, until just thickened. Chill until needed; you can reheat it over a low heat. I like a nice hot slice of apple Charlotte with cold custard.

Hot chocolate and dinky doughnut strips

When it's freezing outside, indulge in this evening treat. Perfect for weekend lazy days, too. Spanish explorers were the first to bring chocolate to Europe in the 16th century and in Spain hot chocolate is often served with churros, a sort of Spanish doughnut.

SERVES 2

HOT CHOCOLATE

- 100G/3½OZ DARK CHOCOLATE (AT LEAST 70% COCOA SOLIDS), BROKEN INTO PIECES
- 350ML/12FL OZ/1½ CUPS WHOLE MILK
- CASTER (SUPERFINE) SUGAR, TO TASTE

DOUGHNUTS

- 150ML/5FL OZ/⅔ CUP WHOLE MILK
- 100G/3½OZ/GENEROUS ¾ CUP PLAIN (ALL-PURPOSE) FLOUR, SIFTED
- 2 EGGS, BEATEN
- VEGETABLE OR SUNFLOWER OIL, FOR DEEP-FRYING
- 50G/1¾OZ/¼ CUP CASTER (SUPERFINE) SUGAR
- 1 HEAPED TSP GROUND CINNAMON

1. To make the doughnuts, put the milk and 6–7 tbsp water in a pan and bring to the boil. Remove from the heat, add the flour and beat with a wooden spoon until smooth. Leave to cool slightly, then gradually beat in enough egg to make a stiff, smooth, glossy mixture: it should drop off the spoon but should not be too runny (you may not need all the egg).

2. Spoon the mixture into a piping bag with a large star nozzle. If you don't have a piping bag, improvise with a sandwich bag with the corner cut off: the hole should be about 2.5cm/1in in diameter.

3. In a large, deep pan, heat the oil to 180°C/350°F, or until a cube of bread browns in 30 seconds (don't get your oil too hot or the doughnuts will burn; test 1 doughnut first). Holding the nozzle over the hot oil, gently squeeze the piping bag and snip off 6–8 strips of the mixture – around 10cm/4in long – using kitchen scissors. Deep-fry for 4–5 minutes, turning occasionally, until crisp and golden brown all over. Using a slotted spoon, lift out onto a baking sheet lined with kitchen paper. Repeat until you have cooked all the mixture.

4. To make the hot chocolate, melt the chocolate in a heatproof bowl over a pan of simmering water, making sure the bottom of the bowl doesn't touch the water. Stir to ensure it is completely melted and smooth. (Alternatively, melt in a microwave on full power in 30-second bursts, stirring after each interval.) Meanwhile, bring the milk to the boil in a small pan. Remove the chocolate from the heat and whisk in a little of the hot milk. Add the remaining milk and whisk until frothy. Pour into warmed mugs and add sugar to taste.

5. Mix the sugar and cinnamon together in a bowl and toss with the doughnuts until lightly coated. Serve for dipping into the hot chocolate while curled up on the sofa.

Bread-and-butter pudding

A version of this recipe appeared in 1723 in The Cook's and Confectioner's Dictionary by John Nott. For this classic British dessert it's essential you use stale bread to get the right texture. Standard white sliced doesn't get stale because of all the additives, but a good farmhouse loaf is perfect. Alternatively, brioche or panettone are both wonderful. The slow cooking is crucial – don't try and rush this in a hot oven.

SERVES 4–6

- 50G/1¾OZ/4 TBSP UNSALTED BUTTER, AT ROOM TEMPERATURE, PLUS EXTRA FOR GREASING
- 500G/1LB 2OZ WHITE BREAD, 2–3 DAYS OLD, SLICED AND CRUSTS REMOVED
- 3 TSP MARMALADE (OPTIONAL)
- 100G/3½OZ SULTANAS (GOLDEN RAISINS) OR RAISINS
- 600ML/20FL OZ/2½ CUPS WHOLE MILK
- 1 VANILLA POD, SLIT LENGTHWAYS, WITH THE SEEDS SCRAPED OUT
- 2 EGGS
- 50G/1¾OZ/¼ CUP SOFT LIGHT BROWN SUGAR
- ½ TSP MIXED SPICE (APPLE PIE SPICE) (OPTIONAL)
- 100G/3½OZ/½ CUP DEMERARA SUGAR

1. Preheat the oven to 150°C/300°F/gas mark 2. Lightly butter a 23 x 13cm/9 x 5in ovenproof dish and butter the slices of bread. Spread the marmalade (if using) over the bread. Cut the bread in half diagonally and lay in the dish, overlapping, with the points facing upward. Scatter the sultanas over the bread.

2. Warm the milk in a pan with the vanilla pod and seeds; turn off the heat and leave to infuse for 5–10 minutes. Remove the pod.

3. Meanwhile, beat the eggs with the light brown sugar.

4. Pour the warm milk over the eggs and sugar, whisking continuously so the eggs don't scramble. Add the spice, then immediately pour the mixture over the bread. If you have time, put the dish in the fridge for 30 minutes to soak the bread. (This isn't essential, sometimes I just whack it straight in the oven).

5. Sprinkle with the demerara. Bake for 1½ hours, then turn up the heat to 180°C/350°F/gas mark 4 and bake for a further 15 minutes, until golden and bubbling. Serve hot or cold, with a scoop of ice cream.

Orange and passion fruit trifle with nut brittle

Trifle is one of the greatest eating pleasures of all time. The textures are heavenly and the flavours are so zingy. My nana made this with clementines at Christmas and I longed for it when they weren't in season. I use oranges and I've made a few other tweaks, such as adding nut brittle. The custard is rich and delicious, so don't scrimp on the eggs – if you're going to do this, do it properly. A cut-glass bowl or trifle dish is essential to show off the layers.

SERVES 8–10

- 1 LARGE ORANGE
- 1 X 20CM/8IN VICTORIA SPONGE (PAGE 81), CUT IN HALF HORIZONTALLY, THEN CUT INTO FINGERS
- 3 TBSP COINTREAU
- 500ML/18FL OZ/2½ CUPS WHIPPING OR DOUBLE CREAM
- 50G/1¾OZ/¼ CUP CASTER (SUPERFINE) SUGAR
- 2 WELL-WRINKLED PASSION FRUITS, SEEDS AND PULP SCOOPED OUT
- 1 HANDFUL OF AMARETTI BISCUITS, LIGHTLY CRUSHED

CUSTARD

- 200ML/7FL OZ/GENEROUS ¾ CUP DOUBLE CREAM
- 200ML/7FL OZ/GENEROUS ¾ CUP WHOLE MILK
- 1 VANILLA POD, SLIT LENGTHWAYS AND SEEDS SCRAPED OUT
- 6 EGG YOLKS
- 50G/1¾OZ/¼ CUP CASTER (SUPERFINE) SUGAR
- 25G/1OZ/2 TBSP CORNFLOUR

NUT BRITTLE

- VEGETABLE OIL, FOR GREASING
- 150G/5½OZ/¾ CUP CASTER (SUPERFINE) SUGAR
- 150G/5½OZ/GENEROUS 1 CUP NUTS (ALMONDS, HAZELNUTS, WALNUTS, OR WHATEVER YOU LIKE), TOASTED

1. First make the custard, as it needs to chill. Put the cream and milk in a pan with the vanilla pod and seeds and bring slowly to the boil.

2. In a large, heatproof bowl, whisk the egg yolks with the sugar and cornflour. Pour the simmering cream and milk mixture over the egg mixture, whisking continuously. Return to the pan over a medium heat and stir continuously until thickened. Remove the vanilla pod and leave to cool.

3. Grate the zest of the orange and set aside. Cut off the skin with a sharp knife, then slice the flesh horizontally into thin round slices. Line your trifle bowl with the orange slices, pushing them up the sides of the bowl if possible, as this makes for a beautiful trifle. Place a single layer of sponge fingers on top of the oranges, pressing down a little as you go. Sprinkle the Cointreau over the sponge.

4. Pour the cooled custard over the sponge, cover with cling film and place in the fridge to firm up for about 1 hour, or until ready to serve.

5. To make the nut brittle, lightly oil a baking sheet. Heat the sugar in a frying pan over a medium heat until it melts and forms a deep amber caramel; this will take 5–7 minutes. Do not stir or the sugar will crystallize, just swirl the pan occasionally to make sure it's caramelizing evenly. Turn off the heat and stir in the nuts to coat them in caramel. Tip the mixture onto the baking sheet and pop it in the fridge for 5–10 minutes, or until set. When it's cold and hard, smash it up or snap off shards of the brittle.

6. Whip the cream, not too stiffly, with the sugar and reserved orange zest. Tumble the cream over the set custard, top with the passion fruit pulp and scatter over the crushed amaretti biscuits and nut brittle.

Auntie Jac's banana pudding

◆◆

The best thing about over-ripe bananas is that they scream 'dessert'. I first tried these flavours as a child. We often ate bananas in butterscotch served with the most awful ice cream. It has stuck with me for two reasons: the flavour combination is a knockout and I hate cheap ice cream. This wicked sticky, rich pudding is extremely quick and easy. It is named after my Auntie Jacqueline, who loved it!

SERVES 4

- 125G/4½OZ/1 CUP PLAIN (ALL-PURPOSE) FLOUR
- 3 TSP BAKING POWDER
- 125G/4½OZ/GENEROUS ½ CUP CASTER (SUPERFINE) SUGAR
- 2 VERY RIPE BANANAS, MASHED
- 200ML/7FL OZ/GENEROUS ¾ CUP MILK
- 1 EGG
- 85G/3OZ/6 TBSP UNSALTED BUTTER, MELTED, PLUS EXTRA FOR GREASING
- CUSTARD, TO SERVE (PAGE 175)

BUTTERSCOTCH SAUCE TOPPING

- 2 RIPE BANANAS, SLICED
- 100G/3½OZ/½ CUP DARK BROWN SUGAR
- 4 TBSP MAPLE SYRUP
- 200ML/7FL OZ/GENEROUS ¾ CUP BOILING WATER

1. Preheat the oven to 180°C/350°F/gas mark 4. Grease a 23 x 13cm/9 x 5in ovenproof dish.

2. Sift the flour and baking powder into a bowl, then add the sugar, mashed banana, milk, egg and melted butter. Mix gently until smooth, then tip into the dish.

3. For the topping, scatter the banana slices over the pudding, followed by the brown sugar, maple syrup and finally the boiling water. Bake for 35 minutes, or until golden and risen.

4. Eat warm, although it's equally good cold but served with hot custard.

Sticky coconut rice pudding

◆◆

Rib-stickingly sweet. My nana made this in huge Pyrex dishes to serve all 20 of us on a Saturday afternoon while we watched the racing on the telly. Like all the recipes handed down to me this is short and sweet: she cooked it to a timescale, not for pleasure, but that doesn't mean you can't enjoy this recipe, as I did. I've updated it by using coconut milk to give it a little twist.

SERVES 8

- ◆ 115G/4OZ/GENEROUS ½ CUP SHORT-GRAIN (PUDDING) RICE
- ◆ 410ML CAN COCONUT MILK
- ◆ 250ML/8FL OZ/1 CUP WHOLE MILK
- ◆ 50G/1¾OZ/¼ CUP CASTER (SUPERFINE) SUGAR
- ◆ 50G/1¾OZ/GENEROUS ½ CUP DESICCATED (DRY UNSWEETENED) COCONUT
- ◆ 1 TSP VANILLA EXTRACT
- ◆ 4 TBSP DEMERARA SUGAR
- ◆ 50G/1¾OZ/2 TBSP UNSALTED BUTTER, PLUS EXTRA FOR GREASING

TO SERVE

- ◆ LIME WEDGES
- ◆ 1 RIPE MANGO, PEELED AND SLICED
- ◆ 3–4 TBSP SOFT BROWN SUGAR

1. Preheat the oven to 150°C/300°F/gas mark 2. Lightly butter an ovenproof dish, about 33 x 25cm/13 x 10in.

2. Put the rice, coconut milk, milk, caster sugar, coconut and vanilla in a saucepan and bring to the boil, stirring occasionally. Pour into the buttered dish, sprinkle with demerara sugar, dot with the butter and bake for 1 hour. Don't stir the rice during this time, as you want a crust to form.

3. Serve warm, with wedges of lime, mango slices and a sprinkling of brown sugar – or simply with a dollop of jam.

INDIVIDUAL RICE PUDDINGS

For a dinner party it's nice to make individual rice puddings; bake them for 45 minutes.

Jam roly-poly

◆◆

A proper old-school dessert, this is probably the only thing that tasted better at school than it does at home. Put a few drops of pink food colouring into your custard for the ultimate back-to-school experience. The old wives would have you hanging the poly in muslin (cheesecloth) suspended quivering above a steam bath for a couple of hours so the pastry stays soft. However, all of my aunties bake it, and so do I. It's a 40-minute job from start to finish, and 35 minutes of that is baking time. In 2010, I made this for 180 people at a secret supper in London, hosted by the fantastic Friday Food Club. Imagine making 6 kilos of suet pastry: I had arms like a sailor by the end of it. Using homemade jam makes a simple dessert something special.

SERVES 6

- ◆ 250G/9OZ/2 CUPS SELF-RAISING FLOUR, PLUS EXTRA FOR DUSTING
- ◆ 50G/1¾OZ/¼ CUP SOFT LIGHT BROWN SUGAR
- ◆ 125G/4½OZ SHREDDED SUET (YOU MAY USE VEGETARIAN SUET)
- ◆ BUTTER, FOR GREASING
- ◆ 5 TBSP RASPBERRY JAM, WARMED

1. Preheat the oven to 200°C/400°F/gas mark 6.

2. Sift the flour into a large bowl, then add the sugar and suet. Add about 6 tbsp cold water and bind everything together. (Don't worry if you add too much – if it's really sticky just add a touch more flour. The dough should be soft but definitely not sticky or it won't roll out.) You can either leave the dough in the fridge until later or use it immediately.

3. Place the dough on a floured work surface and roll out into a 30 x 20cm/12 x 8in rectangle. If you get the dough the right shape, reward yourself with a cup of tea – I can't count the number of times I've had to try and roll up a skewed square.

4. Cut a piece of greaseproof paper about the same size as the dough, then lightly grease it with butter.

5. Brush the dough with the warmed jam, leaving a 1cm/½in border all around. If you don't leave this border, your jam will burst out and burn. Roll the dough up like a Swiss roll. It doesn't matter which end you start with, as long as it's rolled into a plump sausage shape. Roll the pud over to leave the join underneath.

6. Place your jam roly-poly on the buttered paper. Wrap or roll the pudding in the paper, not too tight as the dough will expand. Tie the ends with string. Place the wrapped pudding on a baking sheet and bake for 35 minutes.

7. Remove from the oven, unwrap the paper pyjamas, slice the pudding and serve immediately with ice cream or custard, or eat cold with pouring cream. If you can't finish it all in one sitting, keep it wrapped, on a plate in the fridge.

Brown ale bread

◆◆◆

My uncle Ger – a Sunderland man through and through – is going to kill me for this, but I love Newcastle Brown ale. It lends itself beautifully to this loaf, giving it a deep, luxurious flavour. I add cheese and mustard too. This is perfect dunking bread and is also great with a cheeseboard.

MAKE 2 X 450G/1LB LOAVES, COBS OR PLAITS, OR 8 ROLLS

- ◆ 550ML BOTTLE OF BROWN ALE
- ◆ 4 TSP HONEY
- ◆ 7G DRIED YEAST OR 14G FRESH YEAST
- ◆ 530G/1LB 3OZ/4¼ CUPS STRONG WHITE BREAD FLOUR, PLUS EXTRA FOR DUSTING
- ◆ 325G/11½OZ/2½ CUPS WHOLEMEAL (WHOLE WHEAT) FLOUR
- ◆ 200G/7OZ MATURE CHEDDAR CHEESE, GRATED, PLUS EXTRA FOR SPRINKLING
- ◆ 1½ TSP SALT
- ◆ 2 TSP MUSTARD POWDER
- ◆ VEGETABLE OIL, FOR GREASING

1. Warm the brown ale to tepid in a pan over a low heat. Remove from the heat and dissolve the honey and yeast in the liquid. Set aside for 5 minutes to activate the yeast.

2. If you have a food processor you can use the dough hook for the next stage. Mix the bread flour, wholemeal flour, cheese, salt and mustard powder in a large bowl. Add the yeasty beer mixture and mix well with your hands until you have a soft, slightly sticky dough. If the dough feels dry, add a little water; a wet dough is always better than a dry one and will yield moist, light bread. Using floured hands, knead the dough on a floured work surface for around 10 minutes, until smooth and elastic.

3. Put the dough in a lightly oiled bowl, cover with a tea towel or cling film and leave in a warm, draught-free place for 1 hour, until the dough has doubled in size.

4. After 1 hour, knock back the dough; this means punching it to knock out the air. Shape the bread however you want it: in 2 greased and floured loaf tins, as cob loaves, plaits, or 8 rolls. Place them on a baking sheet, spaced well apart and slash or snip the tops to aid rising. Cover with a tea towel or loose cling film and leave in a warm place for 30–45 minutes, until almost doubled in size.

5. Preheat the oven to its highest temperature. When the bread has had its second rising, sprinkle with a little extra cheese and place in the hot oven.

6. As soon as the bread is in, turn the oven down to 200°C/400°F/gas mark 6. The initial blast of heat develops the crust. (Another bakers' tip for a good crust is to spray water inside the oven as you put the bread in.) If you're making rolls, they will take about 10 minutes to cook; 2 loaves or cobs will take 20 minutes. To test if the bread is done, remove from the oven and tap the bottom of the bread: if it sounds hollow, it's cooked. It will also be a beautiful golden brown.

Chicken and leek pie

◆◆

You can't beat a chicken pie, and there are so many variations: mushroom, bacon, leeks... I've tried them all. Pies were a big family favourite when I was growing up, served in slices like doorstops: nice and thick! Do, please, try making your own pastry: it's so easy! The day after you have a roast chicken, pick the meat from the bones and make this pie.

SERVES 4–6

ROUGH PUFF PASTRY

- 250G/9OZ/2 CUPS PLAIN (ALL-PURPOSE) FLOUR, PLUS EXTRA FOR DUSTING
- PINCH OF SALT
- 125G/4½OZ/GENEROUS ½ CUP UNSALTED BUTTER, FROZEN AND GRATED, PLUS EXTRA FOR GREASING
- 5 TBSP ICE-COLD WATER
- 25G/1OZ/1–2 TBSP BUTTER, MELTED
- 1 EGG, BEATEN

FILLING

- VEGETABLE OIL, FOR FRYING
- 2 SMALL LEEKS, CLEANED AND SLICED
- 1 GARLIC CLOVE, PEELED AND CRUSHED
- HANDFUL OF CHESTNUT (CREMINI) MUSHROOMS, SLICED
- 600G/1LB 5OZ ROASTED CHICKEN MEAT, CHOPPED
- 100ML/3½FL OZ/6–7 TBSP WHITE WINE
- 150ML/5FL OZ/⅔ CUP DOUBLE CREAM
- SPRIG OF FRESH TARRAGON, LEAVES PICKED AND ROUGHLY CHOPPED
- SALT AND FRESHLY GROUND BLACK PEPPER

1. To make the pastry, sift the flour and salt into a bowl and roughly rub in the butter (you should still see lumps of butter). Add the water and bring the pastry together. On a lightly floured surface, roll out the dough into a long rectangle, rolling in one direction only. Fold the dough like a letter, top third down, bottom third up and over the top. Roll out again to its original length and repeat the folding. Wrap in cling film and chill in the fridge for at least 30 minutes. Preheat the oven to 200°C/400°F/gas mark 6.

2. To make the filling, heat a little oil in a large frying pan over a medium heat. Add the leeks and garlic and cook gently for 5–10 minutes, until softened. Turn up the heat and add the mushrooms, then cook for a few minutes, stirring all the time so the leeks don't burn. Add the chicken and stir. Add the wine and bubble over a high heat until slightly reduced. Add the cream and tarragon, bring to the boil, then simmer for 5 minutes, until thickened. Season, then set aside to cool. The mixture should be wet but not sloppy.

3. Remove the pastry from the fridge 5 minutes before you want to use it. Spoon the filling into a 23 x 13cm/9 x 5in pie dish. Roll out the pastry so it is the same shape as your pie dish and about 5cm/2in bigger all round; set aside. Grease the rim of the pie dish with butter. Cut 2cm/¾in wide strips of pastry from around the edge of the rolled-out piece and press them around the rim of the dish. Lightly brush the pastry strips with a little melted butter, then lay the rolled-out pastry on top, sticking pastry to pastry. Knock and crimp the edges: squeeze the top and bottom pieces of pastry together gently until they are joined and sealed.

4. Score the top of the pastry lightly in a criss-cross pattern and brush lightly with beaten egg. Bake for 30–40 minutes, until the pastry is golden. Serve straight from the dish with mashed potatoes and greens.

CHRISTMAS BAKING & GIFTS

◆◆◆◆◆◆◆◆◆◆◆◆◆◆◆◆◆◆◆◆◆◆◆◆

Warm your hands, feet and nose, then turn
on the oven. Christmas is the time we love to
bake. This chapter has lots of classics, plus a
few of my more modern family favourites.
'Indulgence', 'warming' and 'stodge' are my
Christmas baking buzzwords. Most of these
recipes can be made in advance, guaranteeing
you a fabulous fuss-free baking season. You'll
find lots of recipes in this book that can be
boxed up in hampers for Christmas presents.
Go on, give it a go. My greatest indulgence is
Christmas pudding fried in lard, definitely
an annual treat! Merry Christmas!

◆◆◆◆◆◆◆◆◆◆◆◆◆◆◆◆◆◆◆◆◆◆◆◆

Spiced fruit and nut loaf with orange cream

◆◆

Don't have hours to steam a pudding? Get confused by pleating foil and making handles out of string? Then you'll love this wicked alternative to the laborious Christmas pudding – and it packs a punch of flavour and booze! I came up with this recipe when I wanted to demonstrate how easy Christmas cooking can be while also giving the audience the opportunity to taste what I'd baked (and not have to wait six months for it to mature). This baby takes about 90 minutes from start to finish, although it's best if you soak the fruit overnight, or at least a few hours in advance.

MAKES 1 X 900G/2LB LOAF

- 250G/9OZ/2 CUPS DRIED FRUITS, SUCH AS SULTANAS (GOLDEN RAISINS), CURRANTS, GLACÉ (CANDIED) CHERRIES, DRIED APRICOTS, PITTED AND CHOPPED DATES AND FIGS
- JUICE OF 1 ORANGE
- 3 TBSP COINTREAU OR BRANDY
- 100G/3½OZ/GENEROUS ¾ CUP PLAIN (ALL-PURPOSE) FLOUR
- 1 TSP BAKING POWDER
- 1 TSP BICARBONATE OF SODA (BAKING SODA)
- 1 TSP GROUND CINNAMON
- 1 TSP GROUND GINGER
- 1 TSP MIXED SPICE (APPLE PIE SPICE)
- 150G/5½OZ/¾ CUP DARK BROWN SUGAR
- 250G/9OZ/2 CUPS NUTS, (TRY HAZELNUTS, ALMONDS AND/OR WALNUTS), TOASTED AND CHOPPED
- 3 LARGE EGGS
- 1 TSP VANILLA EXTRACT
- 40G/1¼OZ/3 TBSP UNSALTED BUTTER, MELTED, PLUS EXTRA FOR GREASING

1. Soak the dried fruits in the orange juice and Cointreau for several hours.

2. Preheat the oven to 150°C/300°F/gas mark 2. Grease a 23 x 13cm/9 x 5in (900g/2lb) loaf tin and line the bottom with a long strip of baking parchment, leaving the ends overhanging to make it easy to lift the loaf out. Drain the soaked fruit thoroughly and reserve the soaking liquid.

3. Sift the flour, baking powder, bicarbonate of soda and spices into a large bowl. Stir in the sugar and nuts. Add the drained fruit and stir to coat the fruit and nuts in the flour: this will prevent them from sinking in the batter.

4. In a separate bowl, whisk the eggs and vanilla for 2 minutes, or until pale and thick, then add this mixture to the fruit-and-nut mixture. Add the reserved soaking liquid from the fruit and the melted butter and mix until all the fruit and nut pieces are coated with the batter, but do not overbeat or the cake will be heavy. Spread into the prepared tin.

RECIPE CONTINUES OVERLEAF

RECIPE CONTINUED FROM PREVIOUS PAGE

TOPPING

- 55G/2OZ/GENEROUS ¼ CUP SUGAR
- 55G/2OZ/4 TBSP UNSALTED BUTTER
- 2 TBSP GOLDEN SYRUP (LIGHT CORN SYRUP)
- SMALL HANDFULS OF YOUR FAVOURITE TOASTED NUTS AND DRIED FRUITS (TRY HAZELNUTS, BLANCHED ALMONDS AND GLACÉ (CANDIED) CHERRIES)

ORANGE CREAM

- 150ML/5FL OZ/⅔ CUP DOUBLE CREAM
- GRATED ZEST OF 1 ORANGE
- 2–3 TBSP COINTREAU (OPTIONAL)

5. Bake for about 1 hour, or until the batter is golden brown and has come away from the sides of the tin. Check after 40 minutes, and if the loaf is browning too quickly, cover with foil. To test whether the loaf is cooked, insert a skewer into the centre: if it comes out clean the cake is ready; if it comes out with mixture sticking to it, put it back in the oven for 5 minutes and then test again. Leave to cool in the tin.

6. To make the topping, melt the sugar and butter in a pan over a medium-high heat, until bubbling. Turn the heat off and add the syrup, nuts and dried fruit. Lift the loaf out of the tin and spoon the topping over it, letting the juices run down the sides. The loaf can be made up to 2 weeks in advance and stored in an airtight container or wrapped in cling film. It's actually better after a couple of days.

7. To make the orange cream, whip the cream until thick, then stir in the orange zest and Cointreau, if using. Serve the cake with the orange cream.

Oatcakes

◆◆◆

Every Christmas I make these as gifts for my family and neighbours. There's nothing like a homemade biscuit for cheese, especially with good Cheddar. If you are giving these as a gift, wrap them in cellophane and tie with festive ribbons. I usually add them to hampers with a bottle of Port and some chutney.

MAKES 24–30

- 300G/10½OZ/3½ CUPS FINE OATMEAL, PLUS 2 TBSP FOR ROLLING
- GOOD PINCH OF SEA SALT
- ¾ TSP BICARBONATE OF SODA (BAKING SODA)
- 25G/1OZ/2 TBSP UNSALTED BUTTER, COLD AND CUBED, PLUS EXTRA FOR GREASING
- 6–7 TBSP TEPID WATER

1. Preheat the oven to 200°C/400°F/gas mark 6. Lightly grease a baking sheet.

2. Mix the oatmeal, salt and bicarbonate of soda together in a bowl and rub in the butter until it resembles breadcrumbs. You can do this in a food mixer if you like. Add the water and mix to a soft dough. You need to use the dough immediately or it will harden.

3. Scatter 1 tbsp oatmeal over your work surface, roll out the dough to about 5mm/¼in thick, and then scatter the rest of the oatmeal on top. As you roll, use a palette knife, a thin spatula or a long sharp knife to ensure the dough isn't sticking to your work surface; just keep running the knife underneath the dough.

4. Use a 6cm/½in diameter cutter to stamp out the oatcakes and place them on a baking sheet. Bake for 30 minutes, or until golden.

5. Leave to cool completely on a wire rack. Store in an airtight container for up to 2 weeks.

Gold-dust pecan fudge brownies

◆◆◆

All my friends get a box of these for Christmas. There's nothing better than a dense brownie packed with pecans and dusted with gold! Gold lustre dust is available online or from cake craft stores. These make a wonderful gift and are fantastic as a dessert, or if you have people round over Christmas these are great to serve with drinks; be careful, though – your guests might not leave!

MAKES 20–24

- 250G/9OZ/GENEROUS 1 CUP UNSALTED BUTTER
- 200G/7OZ DARK CHOCOLATE (70% COCOA SOLIDS), ROUGHLY CHOPPED
- 75G/2¾OZ COCOA POWDER, SIFTED
- 70G/2½OZ/GENEROUS ½ CUP PLAIN (ALL-PURPOSE) FLOUR, SIFTED
- 1 TSP BAKING POWDER
- 350G/12OZ/1¾ CUPS CASTER (SUPERFINE) SUGAR
- 200G/7OZ/2 CUPS PECANS, TOASTED
- 4 EGGS, BEATEN
- GOLD EDIBLE LUSTRE DUST

1. Preheat the oven to 180°C/350°F/gas mark 4. Line a 33 x 20cm/13 x 8in baking tin with baking parchment.

2. Melt the butter and chocolate together in a large, heatproof bowl over a pan of simmering water, making sure the bottom of the bowl doesn't touch the water. Mix gently, until smooth.

3. In a separate bowl, sift together the cocoa, flour and baking powder. Add the sugar and toasted pecans, making sure the pecans are coated in the flour: this will prevent them from sinking in the batter. Add the dry ingredients to the melted chocolate mixture and stir thoroughly.

4. Add the eggs to the mixture and stir to a silky consistency. Pour into the prepared baking tin and bake for 25 minutes, or until slightly springy to the touch. The brownie will still be wobbly, which is fine – you won't be able to test it with a knife, but it will firm up as it cools. Leave to cool in the tin.

5. When cool, carefully transfer to a large cutting board, dust with the gold powder (I use an old clean blusher brush) and cut into chunky squares.

Red wine pear tart with cinnamon pastry

◆◆

I first made this with regular sweet shortcrust pastry; it was good, but the addition of cinnamon lends warmth to the whole dish, making it perfect for a winter dinner party. The pears are poached in mulled wine, so it really is perfect for Christmas. A dollop of clotted cream sets it off beautifully. If you bake your pastry case in advance, this is a very quick dish to make.

MAKES 1 X 23CM/9IN TART

- 1 X 23CM/9IN BLIND-BAKED SWEET PASTRY CASE (PAGE 17, BUT ADD 2 TSP GROUND CINNAMON AND 25G/1OZ/¼ CUP GROUND ALMONDS WITH THE FLOUR)

POACHED PEARS

- 3 RIPE (BUT NOT OVERRIPE) DESSERT PEARS
- 300ML/10FL OZ/1¼ CUPS RED WINE
- 100G/3½OZ/½ CUP CASTER (SUPERFINE) SUGAR
- 3 TBSP GOLDEN SYRUP (LIGHT CORN SYRUP)
- 1 STICK CINNAMON
- 1 STAR ANISE
- 1 VANILLA POD, SLIT LENGTHWAYS AND SEEDS SCRAPED OUT
- 2 CLOVES
- GRATED ZEST OF 1 CLEMENTINE OR SMALL ORANGE

ALMOND SPONGE FILLING

- 85G/3OZ/6 TBSP UNSALTED BUTTER
- 2 EGGS, PLUS 1 YOLK
- 85G/3OZ/SCANT ½ CUP CASTER (SUPERFINE) SUGAR
- 85G/3OZ/GENEROUS ¾ CUP GROUND ALMONDS

1. To poach the pears, peel them and place them in a pan with the remaining poaching ingredients, including the vanilla pod and seeds. Bring to the boil and simmer, uncovered, until the pears are tender. This should take around 20 minutes; you might need to turn the pears every now and again if they aren't submerged. Remove the pears using a slotted spoon and boil the liquid to reduce until syrupy and thickened; set aside. Cut the pears in half and scoop out the middle tough part – a melon baller is ideal for this. Snip off the stems.

2. Preheat the oven to 180°C/350°F/gas mark 4.

3. To make the filling, melt the butter over a medium heat and cook until it is light brown and smells nutty. Leave to cool. In a bowl, whisk together the eggs, yolk, sugar and almonds for a good few minutes, until light and mousse-like. Slowly pour in the cooled melted butter, whisking as you go.

4. Pour the mixture into the pastry case and top with the pears, cut-side down. Bake for 25 minutes, until the almond sponge is golden and firm to the touch.

5. Serve warm or cold, drizzled with some of the reserved syrup, which will intensify the flavour of the tart.

Cranberry and walnut galette

Cranberries are very festive-looking, and I use them for this centrepiece galette, which I make on Boxing Day for my family get-together. The pastry is rich and buttery, with a crisp and crumbly texture. There's more butter than in a standard shortcrust, but it is Christmas, after all, and the galette is packed with fruits so you can afford a little extra indulgence!

MAKES 1 X 20CM/8IN GALETTE

RICH SWEET PASTRY

- 175G/6OZ/1½ CUPS PLAIN (ALL-PURPOSE) FLOUR, PLUS EXTRA FOR DUSTING
- PINCH OF SALT
- 1 TBSP CASTER (SUPERFINE) SUGAR
- 115G/4OZ/½ CUP UNSALTED BUTTER, COLD AND CUBED
- 2 TBSP ICE-COLD WATER

FILLING

- 400G/14OZ/4 CUPS FRESH CRANBERRIES
- 200G/7OZ/1 CUP CASTER (SUPERFINE) SUGAR
- 70G/2½OZ/⅓ CUP SOFT LIGHT BROWN SUGAR
- 100G/3½OZ/1 CUP WALNUTS, TOASTED AND CHOPPED
- GRATED ZEST OF 1 ORANGE
- 2 TBSP DEMERARA SUGAR

TO SERVE

- ICING (CONFECTIONERS') SUGAR, FOR DUSTING
- WHIPPED CREAM
- COINTREAU (OPTIONAL)

1. Start the day before you want to serve this, as the cranberries are best macerated overnight. I usually do it on Christmas Day morning as I'm preparing the cranberry sauce for dinner. Simply chop the cranberries and toss with the caster and brown sugars. Cover with cling film and leave at room temperature overnight. This stops them being bitter and tough.

2. It's easiest to make the pastry in a food processor: put in the flour, salt, sugar and butter and pulse until the mixture resembles breadcrumbs. Trickle in the water, with the processor running, to form a soft dough. You might need a little more water. Wrap the pastry in cling film and chill for at least 1 hour. You can also make this a day in advance.

3. When you're ready to bake your galette, toss the toasted walnuts and orange zest with the cranberry mixture and set aside. Preheat the oven to 200°C/400°F/gas mark 6. Line a baking sheet with baking parchment.

4. Roll out the pastry on a lightly floured surface, to make a rough circle, around 30cm/12in in diameter. Put the pastry on the baking sheet. Pile the cranberry mixture onto the pastry, leaving a 5cm/2in border around the outside. Fold the border back on top of the cranberries and sprinkle it with the demerara sugar. Cover the cranberries with a circle of foil but make sure the pastry border isn't covered. Bake for 35 minutes, until golden brown and crisp.

5. Serve hot or cold, dusted with icing sugar, with whipped cream and a dash of Cointreau if you like.

My family's Christmas pudding

◆◆◆

People either love or hate Christmas pudding. Even if you're a 'hater', this beauty is worth a try: it's fragrant, zesty, moist and delicious. My Nana Jean always got me and all my cousins to gather in the kitchen to give the mixture a stir and make a wish. I make my puddings in October as they are best after a couple of months maturing and feeding. Feeding is basically plying the pudding with booze: Cointreau and brandy are my favourites, but whisky, rum, cider brandy or even Southern Comfort are all fine. If you didn't get around to it earlier, you can make this pudding just two weeks in advance – but no less, as it really benefits from maturing. This recipe makes two puddings: one to keep and the other to give as a gift, wrapped in cellophane and coloured tissue with handmade labels and a sprig of holly. The best tip I can give you for puddings is to buy reusable plastic pudding bowls with lids – I get them online and they're really inexpensive. The lids mean you don't have to pleat paper and foil and make string handles for the pudding bowls, which is the traditional way but a massive chore.

Family Christmas 1981. Mam second right pregnant with me!

**MAKES 2 X 2-LITRE/3½-PINT/
9-CUP PUDDINGS**

- 800G/1LB 12OZ MIXED DRIED FRUITS
  SUCH AS SULTANAS (GOLDEN RAISINS),
  RAISINS AND CURRANTS
- 500G/1LB 2OZ DATES (EITHER
  FRESH MEDJOOL OR DRIED
  READY-TO-EAT), CHOPPED
- 3–4 TBSP RUM
- 125G/4½OZ/1 CUP PLAIN
  (ALL-PURPOSE) FLOUR
- 2 TSP GROUND CINNAMON
- 2 TSP ALLSPICE
- 2 TSP GRATED NUTMEG
- 250G/9OZ SUET (BEEF
  OR VEGETARIAN)
- 200G/7OZ/4 CUPS BREADCRUMBS
- 450G/1LB/2¼ CUPS SOFT DARK
  BROWN SUGAR
- 2 CRISP DESSERT APPLES, SUCH AS
  COX'S, GRATED
- GRATED ZEST OF 1 ORANGE
- 100G/3½OZ/1 CUP SLIVERED
  ALMONDS, TOASTED
- 300ML/10FL OZ/1¼ CUPS STOUT
- 5 EGGS, BEATEN
- BUTTER, FOR GREASING
- BRANDY, WHISKY, RUM, COINTREAU OR
  SOUTHERN COMFORT (YOUR CHOICE,
  BUT IT NEEDS TO BE ABOUT 40% ABV)
- BRANDY BUTTER, CREAM OR CUSTARD,
  TO SERVE

1. Start the day before you want to make your pudding. Put the dried fruits, including the dates, in a really large bowl (the largest you have) and pour over the rum.

2. The next day, sift the flour and spices over the fruit, then add the suet, breadcrumbs, sugar, apples, orange zest and almonds. Mix thoroughly.

3. In a separate bowl or jug, measure out the stout then add the eggs and whisk together. Pour over the pudding mixture and mix well; the mixture should be sloppy and should fall from the spoon when tapped – if it's still a bit thick add a little more stout.

4. Grease 2 x 2-litre pudding bowls lightly. Fill the bowls no more than three-quarters full, as the mixture will expand as it cooks. Place a circle of greaseproof paper on top of the mixture and then put the lids on the bowls, making sure they are clipped on tightly.

5. Now you need to steam the puddings for 6 hours. If you don't have a steamer, put a trivet or a small heatproof dish in 2 pans, then half-fill the pans with boiling water, lower the puddings into the water, cover the pans with a well-fitting lid and steam over a low heat for 6 hours. If you don't have well-fitting lids you can use foil, as long as it's tightly sealed and no steam can escape. You'll need to top up the water every hour, using boiling water from the kettle. After 6 hours, carefully remove the puddings from the water and leave at room temperature to cool completely.

6. Remove the greaseproof paper and make small holes all over the pudding with a skewer. To give the pudding its first 'feed', pour over a few tablespoons of your chosen booze, then cover the pudding with a clean circle of greaseproof paper and replace the lid. Store in a cool, dark, dry place until Christmas, feeding once a week with more alcohol.

7. The quickest way to reheat this on Christmas Day is in the microwave. Remove the lid and replace loosely, then microwave on full power for 6 minutes, until piping hot in the middle. Alternatively, steam it for a further 45 minutes. Test it with a skewer. Serve hot, with brandy butter, cream or custard – or all three!

Boxing Day muffins

◆◆◆

One of our great family traditions is the Christmas muffin, which is always made on Boxing Day when there's tons of leftover Christmas pudding in the fridge. These are so simple that you can whip them up in 30 minutes flat. They are the perfect accompaniment to an afternoon movie in your new Christmas pyjamas.

MAKES 6 LARGE MUFFINS

◆ 1 EGG
◆ 125ML/4FL OZ/½ CUP BUTTERMILK
◆ 125G/4½OZ/1 CUP PLAIN
  (ALL-PURPOSE) FLOUR
◆ 1 TSP BAKING POWDER
◆ 1 TSP MIXED SPICE (PUMPKIN PIE SPICE)
◆ 85G/3OZ/SCANT ½ CUP CASTER
  (SUPERFINE) SUGAR
◆ 125G/4½OZ LEFTOVER
  CHRISTMAS PUDDING
◆ 25G/1OZ/2 TBSP UNSALTED
  BUTTER, MELTED
◆ 2 TBSP BRANDY OR WHISKY
◆ ICING (CONFECTIONERS') SUGAR,
  FOR DUSTING

1. Preheat the oven to 190°C/375°F/gas mark 5. Line a non-stick muffin tin with large paper muffin cases.

2. Whisk the egg and buttermilk together. Sift the flour and baking powder into a bowl, then add the spice and sugar. Crumble in the Christmas pudding.

3. Beat, slowly adding the egg mixture, then the melted butter and brandy. The mixture should be lumpy, so don't overbeat, just gently stir. It's fine to have traces of dry mixture. Fill the muffin cases almost full.

4. Bake for 25 minutes, until well risen and springy to the touch. Leave to cool in the tin for a few minutes, then transfer to a wire rack.

5. Dust with icing sugar and enjoy within 24 hours. Christmas pudding never tasted so good!

Gingerbread Christmas tree decorations

◆◆

These are such fun and are a big family tradition. Don't forget to buy some ribbon or yarn for them! They look stunning hung on the Christmas tree and are a great idea for your kids to take to school on the last day of term for their friends. I give all my neighbours these on Christmas Eve.

MAKES AT LEAST 24, DEPENDING ON CUTTERS AND SHAPES

◆ 225G/8OZ/1 CUP UNSALTED BUTTER, PLUS EXTRA FOR GREASING

◆ 175G/6OZ/GENEROUS ¾ CUP SOFT LIGHT BROWN SUGAR

◆ 175G/6OZ/½ CUP GOLDEN SYRUP (LIGHT CORN SYRUP)

◆ 550G/1LB 4OZ/4½ CUPS PLAIN (ALL-PURPOSE) FLOUR, PLUS EXTRA FOR DUSTING

◆ 1 TSP BICARBONATE OF SODA (BAKING SODA)

◆ 3 TSP GROUND GINGER

◆ 1 TSP GROUND CINNAMON

TO DECORATE

◆ ICING (CONFECTIONERS') SUGAR

◆ FOOD COLOURINGS

◆ SPRINKLES, DRAGEES AND EDIBLE GLITTER

1. Preheat the oven to 180°C/350°F/gas mark 4. Grease a large baking sheet.

2. Melt the butter, sugar and syrup together in a pan over a medium heat. Bring to the boil, then remove from the heat. Sift together the flour, bicarbonate of soda and spices. Beat this mixture into the butter-and-sugar mixture, until smooth. Tip the dough out onto cling film, then wrap and chill for 10 minutes.

3. Roll out the dough on a lightly floured surface to about 1cm/½in thick. Cut out the shapes. You can reroll the scraps and cut out more shapes to use all the dough if you wish.

4. Bake for 12–15 minutes. The cookies will still be soft when they come out of the oven, but they harden as they cool: don't be tempted to cook them until they are solid. As soon as they come out of the oven, stamp or press a hole in the top of each shape for the ribbon to go through. Leave to cool on a rack.

5. To decorate, make a runny but spreadable icing with icing sugar and boiling water, colour as you choose and spoon over the cookies. Decorate with sprinkles, dragees or glitter and leave to dry.

6. Slot the ribbon through the holes and hang on your Christmas tree. Glitter gives a fantastic effect as it catches the light when they are on the tree. Beautiful.

Florentines

These traditional thin almond and fruit biscuits are a doddle to make. They are great to offer guests and I always have a plateful on my coffee table on Christmas Eve. At the bakery we make hundreds for our hampers, too, gift-wrapped with holly and a candy cane. Make sure you follow this recipe precisely though: Florentines are temperamental.

MAKES ABOUT 12

- 25G/1OZ/2 TBSP UNSALTED BUTTER
- 150G/5½OZ/¾ CUP CASTER (SUPERFINE) SUGAR
- 35G/1¼OZ/3 TBSP PLAIN (ALL-PURPOSE) FLOUR
- 125ML/4FL OZ/½ CUP CRÈME FRAÎCHE
- 115G/4OZ/GENEROUS 1 CUP SLIVERED ALMONDS, TOASTED
- 100G/3½OZ/GENEROUS ½ CUP DRIED FRUITS, SUCH AS CHERRIES, CURRANTS, DATES
- 3 TBSP PRESERVED GINGER, FINELY CHOPPED
- 200G/7OZ DARK, MILK OR WHITE CHOCOLATE, BROKEN INTO PIECES

1. Preheat the oven to 180°C/350°F/gas mark 4. Line a baking sheet with baking parchment.

2. Melt the butter and sugar in a pan over a low-medium heat, bring to the boil, then remove from the heat. Beat in the flour and crème fraîche, then stir in the almonds, dried fruits and ginger. Leave to stand at room temperature for 10 minutes to thicken; if your kitchen is particularly warm, put the pan in the fridge for the first 5 minutes.

3. Put heaped teaspoons of the mixture on the baking sheet, spaced 5cm/2in apart to allow the Florentines to spread; don't flatten them. Bake for 15 minutes, until golden brown. Cool on a wire rack.

4. Melt the chocolate in a heatproof bowl set over a bowl of simmering water, making sure the bottom of the bowl doesn't touch the water, then remove from the heat. Dip the Florentines in the melted chocolate and leave to dry, chocolate-side up. If you like, you can add a squiggle with the prongs of a fork.

My mam in the late 70s

PS...

When I'm not in the kitchen, my big passions are the Mod and Northern soul scenes, two British subcultures that were spawned more than 20 years before I was born. I got into Oasis in 1994, and from researching their influences I learned about Paul Weller and The Rolling Stones. Looking back into their musical tastes, I picked up on soul and R'nB, with artists like Muddy Waters and Bo Diddley. I'll never forget hearing the Rolling Stones singing 'Paint it Black' on the radio when I was about 13. My Uncle Norman gave me a 'Beggars Banquet' first-pressing vinyl shortly afterwards and I was hooked. The soul, the passion, the music: I adored everything about the band, especially Brian Jones.

The Mod and Northern soul scenes, although intrinsically linked via music, are completely separate. Being a Mod to me is about 'clean living under difficult circumstances' (the words of Pete Meaden, one of the most influential figures in the Mod subculture); making every detail count and making the best of how you look and what you have. It's more than fashion, it's how I live, how I feel, what I cook, my morals, my personality. I've been a Mod since I was 15. I got it wrong at first, but gradually, by reading books, watching documentaries, asking people who'd been there at the start, I got there. I love going out and meeting other people into Mod culture. A similar taste in music, clothes and lifestyle are great bonding tools.

Northern soul is purely about music and dancing: I don't think dress comes into it, although there are a few favourites among the diehards, such as Oxford bags and circle skirts. Imagine 2,000 people plus, dancing to DJs spinning vinyl that was recorded and pressed up to 60 years ago, music that pins you to the wall with its beat. Big floor stompers with amazing breaks such as The Vibrations' ''Cause you're mine'. You can't help but be intrigued. No-one drinks heavily, because being drunk inhibits your dancing ability; everything is secondary to the music.

Index

Thank you

Mam, who has given me everything since the day I was born: you make so, so proud to be your daughter. Everything good in me comes from you and you've done it all yourself.

Nana Jean, for spending countless days in the kitchen with me, teaching me and letting me make mistakes without telling me off. You started this journey for me and I will be eternally grateful.

My friends Leila, Tori, Adam, Ryan, Kristian, Kate, Nick, John and Chris, for your support and friendship, and for the laughter and tears. You're my crew and always will be. How do you eat yours?

Aunties, uncles and cousins, for the best childhood memories.

Katherine, my agent, for believing in me in the early days and for your positive attitude; you said from day one this is where we would be and you were right!

Becca, my publisher, for giving me a chance, and for being lovely to work with and listening to my ideas.

The wonderful Dan Jones and his lovely assistant Andrew, the Paul Daniels and Debbie McGee of the photography world. Thanks for listening to my ideas and not laughing at my 'TV smile'.

Karin Fremer for capturing my spirit in her designs.

Tori, remember the first beehive you did upstairs at your dad's? How small was it? I hope you and The Black Door Salon continue to grow and prosper. You are the only one I trust with my hair.

ND Make-up artists, for the best flash lashes ever! You always do my make-up flawlessly and you're such great girls.

Mac, for the flawless make-up, which has helped create my signature look. SNOB addict!

Art Gallery Clothing (www.artgalleryclothing.co.uk). Thank you Alex for the most stylish threads and accessories. Always a pleasure to be seen in Art Gallery.

Sam and Kev Roberts, I'm humbled to call you friends, and am so happy we met. If it wasn't for you both and GoldSoul my social life would be rubbish!

Latimers fish deli in Sunderland for the best fish and advice in the North. Wicked people, amazing fish and a great atmosphere.

Helen Little, of Helen Russell Photography, Sunderland. For being a good friend and a flawless photographer. Thanks for the portraits on pages 7, 23, 30, 118 and 205; you took my ideas and produced something beyond my expectations.

KitchenAid, for making baking a pure pleasure. Magimix, for saving me hours grating carrots for my carrot cake.

The Rolling Stones, for making me believe there was something better out there for me and forging me into a confident woman.

The people of Sunderland for their support since MasterChef, especially The Sunderland Echo.

Percy, my baby boy, for cheering me up when things get hard and for always making me smile. One day we will win Crufts.

Stacie Stewart first came to public attention when she reached the finals of *Masterchef* in 2010, and she is now judge and mentor for the baking category on the ITV's *food.Glorious.food.* Her bakery, *The Beehive Bakery*, supplies both modern and vintage-style cakes and bakes to shops and events all over the country.